IMAGES
of America

WAYNESVILLE

MAIN STREET. For more than a century, events have taken place on the Haywood County Courthouse lawn (center left behind trees) on Main Street. In this *c.* 1910 photograph, local residents arrive in horse-drawn buggies and automobiles for a festive occasion that may have been a Fourth of July or Decoration Day event. (Courtesy of Haywood County Public Library Digital Collection.)

ON THE COVER: TRAIN COMES TO WAYNESVILLE. The first train arrived in Waynesville in April 1883, after westward rail lines were laid through Canton and Clyde to the east. The No. 634 steam train, pictured here, rolled into the town's depot in present-day Frog Level. By the middle of the 20th century, the automobile had superseded the train as the main form of transportation. The last passenger train to Waynesville came in 1949. (Courtesy of Sara Martin.)

IMAGES
of America

WAYNESVILLE

Michael Beadle and Peter Yurko

ARCADIA
PUBLISHING

Published by Arcadia Publishing
Charleston, South Carolina

Library of Congress Control Number: 2010922719

For all general information contact Arcadia Publishing at:
Telephone 843-853-2070
Fax 843-853-0044
E-mail sales@arcadiapublishing.com
For customer service and orders:
Toll-Free 1-888-313-2665

Visit us on the Internet at www.arcadiapublishing.com

From Peter: For Nancy
From Michael: For Nicole

CONTENTS

Acknowledgments   6

Introduction   7

1.   Early History   9

2.   People of Waynesville   23

3.   Steeples and Students   47

4.   Open for Business   61

5.   Hazelwood   79

6.   Tourism   99

7.   Arts and Leisure   113

Bibliography   127

ACKNOWLEDGMENTS

This book would not be possible without the generous support of the Haywood County Public Library (HCPL), the Haywood County Historical and Genealogical Society, and the many Waynesville and Haywood County residents who graciously shared collections of historic photographs and invaluable history about Waynesville and its people. A special thanks goes to the staff at the HCPL—especially librarian Joyce Cope for her patience, diligence, and willingness to scan most of the photographs found in this book. Through HCPL's efforts and leadership of executive director Robert Busko, future generations will be able to enjoy a huge historic collection of images that few counties of its size can boast. Many thanks as well go to Henry Foy, Bruce Briggs, George Frizzell, Vicki Hyatt, Lee Starnes, Laura Soltis, Jackie Stephens, Bette Sprecher, Kathy Ross, Louise K. Nelson, Bobby Joe McClure, Rolf Kaufman, Steve Lloyd, Kay Miller, Lynn Noland, Lin Forney, Lee and Lorraine Bouknight, Mike McKinney, Mary Ann Enloe, Bo Prevost, Mary Greer, Wells Greeley, Ron Muse, Kimberly Crowe, Ernest Klatt, Sara Martin, and many others who supplied us with photographs or postcards for this project. We hope the unique images captured in this book will spur others in the community to preserve and share their own collections of historic photographs and documents, so we may continue to explore the rich veins of local history.

INTRODUCTION

Long before the town of Waynesville came into existence, Cherokees inhabited the area for centuries, hunting and farming. In the 1500s, Spanish explorers passed through the region in search of gold, but finding none, they moved on south and west. In the 1600s and 1700s, English and French hunters found plenty of wild game during travels through the area, but no permanent white settlements were made in western North Carolina until the late 18th century.

In July 1776, Cherokee warriors attacked American settlements in western North Carolina. In August, a militia of 2,400 men led by Gen. Griffith Rutherford marched into what is now Haywood County and present-day Waynesville, burning villages, destroying crops, and capturing or killing any who resisted. The military campaign sought to crush pro-British support that some Cherokee villages harbored against a fledgling American rebellion. Taking a route that would later become known as the Rutherford Trace, the men entered Haywood County from the east, moved through present-day Canton, forded the Pigeon River in Bethel, and made their way to Richland Creek near what is now downtown Waynesville. The soldiers, mostly frontier men from North Carolina's western region, as well as Catawba Indian scouts, camped along Richland Creek before marching on past the Balsam Mountains and destroying dozens of Cherokee villages. Meeting little resistance, they retraced this route on their way back east that same month.

After the war, many of these soldiers made their way back along the Rutherford Trace to claim land in western North Carolina. The Cherokee, decimated by disease and famine, were pushed farther west as treaties and land speculation opened more land to white settlements. By the 1790s, a small community known as Mount Prospect had formed near Richland Creek. Col. Robert Love, a Revolutionary War officer from Virginia, settled in this community and soon acquired vast amounts of land. Thomas Love, his younger brother, wrote a bill that passed through the North Carolina legislature to create Haywood County in December 1808. Local leaders met the following year to form a government, build a courthouse and roads, and carry out the business of the new county. Robert Love, elected as the county's first clerk of court, donated 17 acres of his property to create what would become Waynesville's downtown district. Lots were sold to help pay for the construction of a new county courthouse. Love suggested the town be called Waynesville in honor of the Revolutionary War general "Mad" Anthony Wayne.

Waynesville grew very slowly in its first several decades. Without railroad lines or major roads, the town was little more than a farming community with stores, churches, and family homes. The county's first courthouse opened in 1812 in the Town Square (near the present-day town hall). Main Street was a dirt road with a few side roads leading to other farming communities in the county. In its early days, Waynesville operated three taverns, including the Battle House (located next to the present-day town hall). There was a small slave population in Waynesville. Wealthy landowners, such as the Love family, owned dozens of slaves. By the mid-1800s, the main occupation was still farming, but there were also blacksmiths, millers, carpenters, teachers, doctors, and various merchants.

By the outbreak of the Civil War in 1861, Waynesville still had dirt roads, no major industry, and no railroad lines. When North Carolina seceded from the Union in May 1861, scores of Waynesville men marched off to war in locally formed Confederate regiments. R. G. A. Love, a grandson of Robert Love, organized the county's first volunteer unit—Company L of North Carolina's 16th Regiment. While battles raged in far-off towns and cities, Waynesville was not immune to the deprivations of war. Robbed of many of their men, families struggled to keep farms and businesses going. Mountain communities were subject to vigilante gangs that roamed the countryside, terrorizing residents, stealing livestock, and robbing homes of food. Near the end of the war, in February 1865, six-hundred Union raiders led by Col. George Kirk, stormed into Waynesville, ransacked local houses, burned the home of Col. Robert Love, emptied the jail, and set it aflame before racing back into Tennessee with plunder and prisoners.

A month after Gen. Robert E. Lee surrendered his Confederate army at Appomattox, pockets of resistance remained in western North Carolina. In fact, the last shot of the Civil War east of the Mississippi River is said to have been fired just outside of Waynesville, near present-day Sulphur Springs Road. On May 6, 1865, a Union regiment led by Col. William C. Bartlett met a Confederate unit of sharpshooters, and in the ensuing skirmish, one Union soldier was killed. When Union and Confederate leaders met at the Battle House the next day, each side agreed to a truce, ending hostilities in the region.

Waynesville officially incorporated as a town in 1871. Transportation lines slowly improved. A stagecoach operated between Asheville and Waynesville in the 1870s. In 1878, William Williams Stringfield and his wife, Maria, opened a resort just outside of town called the White Sulphur Springs Hotel. By 1882, railroad lines finally arrived in the county, bringing a surge of commerce and people. Timber companies and sawmills began to flourish throughout the county. The Junaluska Leather Company opened just west of Waynesville in 1897. At the turn of the century, Pennsylvanian businessman E. E. Quinlan moved to the area and opened the Quinlan-Monroe Lumber Company. A village known as Quinlantown cropped up along Allen's Creek in the years that followed. The Unagusta Furniture Company, an offshoot of Quinlan's lumber operation, opened in 1904. The growing industrial community officially became the town of Hazelwood in 1905 with E. E. Quinlan serving as its first mayor. By the mid-1900s, Hazelwood had become a thriving industrial hub for factories producing furniture, textiles, rubber products, and shoes.

In the 1900 census, Waynesville—the county's largest town—only boasted 1,307 people. By 1950, Waynesville's population grew to 5,295 and retook the lead as the county's largest town and steadily grew to nearly 7,500 residents by 1990. It expanded even more when Hazelwood merged with Waynesville in 1995.

Though the town has maintained a relatively small size over two centuries, Waynesville continues to swell each summer thanks to its reputation as a popular tourist destination. Dating back to the late 1800s, summer guests from big cities all along the Eastern Seaboard came to Waynesville to savor cool mountain air, scenic vistas, and small-town charm. They would stay for weeks or even months. Servants and wait staff from Southern states also came, earning steady pay over the summer seasons. Physicians touted the healing qualities of mineral springs and cool air as remedies for skin disorders and respiratory diseases. Waynesville's influx of cosmopolitan guests also encouraged the local arts and culture scene. Guests could enjoy elegant parties, fine dining, formal dancing, and lawn croquet. Dozens of homes were converted into summer boardinghouses. Others expanded to become inns and grand hotels such as the Eagle's Nest, the Bon Air Hotel, Suyeta Park Hotel, the Gordon, the Dunham House, and the Kenmore Hotel. Most of these hotels gradually lost business to cheaper motels and interstate travel. They were eventually demolished to make room for other businesses. Others were destroyed by fire.

Throughout its history, Waynesville has welcomed many famous figures, from Franklin and Eleanor Roosevelt to Hollywood actor Gig Young. The town has also produced a pair of congressmen, the state's first All-American football player, and many artists, entrepreneurs, and scholars. What follows in these pages is a sampling of the people, places, and events that helped shape a unique mountain town that has endured and prospered for two centuries.

One

EARLY HISTORY

LAND SALE. Waynesville remained a sparsely populated village for decades after its founding in 1810. When train service came in the 1880s, more people came looking to buy land. The lots for sale in this scene from the early 1900s included plots overlooking present-day Wall Street, Welch Street, and East Street. (Courtesy of Henry Foy.)

ROBERT LOVE. The son of Samuel and Dorcas Bell Love, Robert Love was born near the Tinkling Spring Meeting House in Augusta County, Virginia, on May 11, 1760. During the Revolutionary War, he joined Virginia's Patriot militia and fought in battles throughout the war. Afterwards, he moved to present-day northeast Tennessee and later to what would become Waynesville in the 1790s. He became Haywood County's first clerk of court and amassed a fortune through land speculation and surveying in western North Carolina. In 1809, he donated 17 acres to create the present-day downtown Waynesville district and suggested the name Waynesville in honor of Gen. "Mad" Anthony Wayne. A wealthy slave owner and a political patriarch of the county, Love is described in some accounts as wearing a blue swallow-tail coat, knee breeches, silver knee buckles, and silk stockings. He served on the state's electoral college in presidential elections from 1804 to 1832 and helped survey the border between North Carolina and Tennessee. While on a trip to see relatives in Tennessee, Love was kicked by a horse. The injury left him with a limp for the rest of his life. He died in 1845 and is buried at Green Hill Cemetery in Waynesville. (Courtesy of HCPL Digital Collection.)

GEN. "MAD" ANTHONY WAYNE. A Pennsylvania-born officer and statesman, Anthony Wayne earned his odd moniker for being hot-tempered and a strict disciplinarian. During the Revolutionary War, he led the capture of a British fort at Stony Point on the Hudson River. After the war, as commander-in-chief of the U.S. Army, he defeated a confederation of Native Americans in a series of battles along the Ohio River that culminated in the Battle of Fallen Timbers in 1794. Many towns, counties, businesses, schools, and streets in the Eastern and Midwestern United States are named after this general, including Fort Wayne, Indiana, and Waynesville, North Carolina. In fact, the names of Bruce Wayne (the alter ego of Batman), and John Wayne (the stage name for the great cowboy actor), both derive their last names from Anthony Wayne. (Courtesy of HCPL Digital Collection.)

FARMLAND PANORAMA. Early white settlers found rich, fertile river valleys in Haywood County including land along Richland Creek, which flows through Waynesville, seen here in the foreground. In the late 18th century, land speculators bought up and surveyed thousands of acres of land in the area and became powerful leaders in a cash-poor, land-rich society. Families and enterprising individuals moved into the area from all directions. Waynesville's early name, Mount Prospect,

and Richland Creek are just a few examples of the place names that suggest the opportunity this frontier land offered settlers. At center, standing high on the ridge overlooking the valley in this *c*. 1892 photograph is the old brick Haywood County Courthouse, built in 1884. (Courtesy of Hunter Library, Western Carolina University.)

EARLY HAYWOOD COURTHOUSE. Haywood County has had five courthouses during its history. The first structure, completed in 1812, had a frame post-and-beam construction and stood at the Town Square, approximately where the present-day Waynesville Town Hall building stands. This structure was then replaced by a second building in 1844, erected on the corner of Main and East Streets, about where the present-day Waynesville Police Department stands. The third courthouse, completed in 1884, was a brick building (pictured above), which stood at the corner of Main and Depot Streets on the present-day courthouse lot. By 1928, a state building inspector condemned the building as unsafe, and it was torn down—but only after a 1931 grand jury issued an indictment against Haywood County commissioners for ignoring their duties to build a newer, safer courthouse. (Courtesy of Hunter Library, Western Carolina University.)

MODERN HAYWOOD COURTHOUSE. The Charlotte architectural firm of Rogers and Rhodes designed the county's fourth courthouse, pictured here, completed in 1932. Built during the Great Depression in the neoclassical style that was popular at the time, the three-story building included ground-floor windows with arched tops and classical features like Doric columns and a triangular pediment decorating the front side. This courthouse underwent recent renovations and reopened in 2009. In 2004, the county opened its fifth courthouse, known as the Haywood County Justice Center, where present-day court proceedings are held. (Courtesy of the *Mountaineer*.)

ORDER IN THE COURT. A bas-relief of the Scales of Justice (center, rear) appears behind the judge's bench in what was once the Haywood County Courthouse's main courtroom, where criminal trials, civil court proceedings, political events, county meetings, and holiday events took place from the early 1930s to the 21st century. Today the room serves primarily as a site for monthly Haywood County commissioner meetings. (Courtesy of Henry Foy.)

DOWNTOWN, 1886. The scene above shows the north end of Main Street from atop the Haywood County Courthouse. The steepled First Presbyterian Church of Waynesville stands in the center on the left side of the road. The tall house directly across the street from the church is Alden Howell's family home, which later became the site for the Gordon Hotel. By the early 1900s, the town saw a steady rise in population and building. (Courtesy of Henry Foy.)

DOWNTOWN, 1910. The photograph above reveals new homes and businesses (including the Windsor Hotel in the left foreground), street improvements, sidewalks, and electric power lines. Note the updated First Presbyterian Church. (Courtesy of Henry Foy.)

FROG LEVEL SCENE. The Frog Level district of Waynesville was hopping with business in the early 1900s thanks to a train depot that welcomed visitors seeking summer vacations in the mountains. In 1918, a military hospital set up at the nearby White Sulphur Springs Hotel brought in another wave of visitors, including soldiers recovering from gas attacks and respiratory illnesses after World War I. The old armory building stands behind the car, and the old Massie Furniture building stands in the back right. (Courtesy of Henry Foy.)

CONFEDERATE VETERANS REUNION. Haywood County lost 251 of the 1,126 county men who served in the Civil War. Many died in Union prisons. For many years, to honor fallen comrades and remember those who returned from battle, Confederate veterans held annual reunions, as seen in this 1910 gathering in front of the Haywood County Courthouse. From left to right are (first row) Jim Milliner, John Mill, Marion Smathers, unidentified, John Caldwell, Anderson Singleton, John Singleton, Columbus Singleton (the Singleton brothers served in the same regiment, Company F of the 25th North Carolina Regiment, and were known affectionately as "the Three

Musketeers"), Dick Moody, Archibald Justice, John McGee, unidentified, Jim Edwards, Mat Parton, Henry Burress, Atlas Allen, Lawson Messer, and M. D. Kinsland; (second row) Alex Carpenter, John L. Morrow, James Morrow, two unidentified, Wylie Caldwell, Joshua H. Allison, Merritt Trantham, Mark Killian, unidentified, William Thomas Price, Lush V. Welch, Hack Hargrove, R. L. Underwood, Bill Bennett, Western Green, unidentified, James Swayngim, unidentified, Calvin Cagle, unidentified, Taylor McClure, and Jake Evans. (Courtesy of the Haywood County Historical and Genealogical Society.)

19

MUDDY STREETS. Waynesville's early dirt roads often frustrated travelers, especially during rainy seasons, as seen in this photograph from the early 1900s. With the birth of the automobile and its rising popularity, local residents pushed for improved roads. In 1905, the town began resurfacing Main Street with bricks. (Courtesy of HCPL Digital Collection.)

CURBSIDE PARKING. While motorized transportation brought about road improvements, including brick streets, curbs, and sidewalks, residents continued to use yoked oxen and carts as seen here on Main Street. The tree-shaded home in the background was formerly a boardinghouse and is the present-day site of Mast General Store. (Courtesy of Henry Foy.)

POWER LINES. As Waynesville neared its centennial, Main Street included merchant shops, private homes, boardinghouses, and churches. In 1903, the Haywood Electrical Power Company began, modernizing the town with light and electricity from rows of power lines. (Courtesy of HCPL Digital Collection.)

SIDE STREET. Late-19th-century Waynesville residents traveled by wagons pulled by horses or yoked oxen. George Sherrill, second from left, would later become a prominent photographer in the county, operating a studio on Depot Street in downtown Waynesville in the early 1900s. His mother is second from right. Local historians are working on digitally restoring a vast collection of Sherrill Studio glass slides housed at the Shelton House Museum in Waynesville. (Courtesy of Henry Foy.)

PIGEON STREET. Once a quiet, tree-lined avenue heading out of town, this road leads to the Bethel community. Travelers pass the historic Shelton House, Haywood Arts Regional Theatre, the Salvation Army building, Mount Olive Missionary Baptist Church, the Pigeon Street Community Development Center (formerly a segregated school for African Americans), and the Jones Temple AME Zion Church. (Courtesy of Henry Foy.)

EAST STREET. Formerly known as Cross Street because it crossed through Town Square in the center of downtown Waynesville, East Street earned a new name to denote its direction as the Town Square evolved and the early Haywood County Courthouse moved farther down the street to its present-day location. Even into the 1920s, as shown here, the street was a dirt road flanked by several houses. (Courtesy of Henry Foy.)

Two

PEOPLE OF WAYNESVILLE

SAMUEL L. LOVE. A grandson of Col. Robert Love and a prominent Waynesville physician and politician, Samuel Love (1828–1887) served as the state's auditor from 1877 to 1881. He was the first person from Haywood County to hold a statewide post. Active in politics before, during, and after the Civil War, he won a seat as a state representative in the North Carolina General Assembly in 1856 and was reelected each term through the end of the war. He also served as the surgeon for Gov. John Ellis and Gov. Zebulon Vance. (Courtesy of HCPL Digital Collection.)

WILLIAM HOLLAND THOMAS. Though he was born in 1805 just outside of Waynesville and never technically lived within the town limits, William Holland Thomas is forever linked with Waynesville. His legion of Cherokee and mountaineer Confederate troops agreed to a truce with Union forces in downtown Waynesville at the Battle House on May 8, 1865, marking one of the final Confederate surrenders ending the Civil War. Thomas began work as a clerk in a trading post near present-day Maggie Valley. Adopted by a Cherokee leader named Drowning Bear, who dubbed the young man Wil-Usdi, or "Little Will," Thomas taught himself the finer points of law and grew to become a prominent businessman, attorney, and state legislator. In Washington, D.C., he pursued land claims on behalf of the Cherokee nation and secured the tracts that became the Qualla Boundary, which is the present-day home of the Eastern Band of Cherokee Indians. Thomas died in 1893 and is buried in Waynesville's Green Hill Cemetery. (HCPL Digital Collection.)

WILLIAM WILLIAMS STRINGFIELD. Born in Strawberry Plains, Tennessee, W. W. Stringfield joined the Confederate army at the start of the Civil War and helped recruit members for the Thomas Legion, led by William Holland Thomas. Stringfield fought in numerous battles and rose to the rank of major before he was eventually captured and imprisoned in Knoxville at the end of the war. After his release, he moved to Waynesville, married, and operated the White Sulphur Springs Hotel, which became a prominent resort in Haywood County. As a state senator, Stringfield fought to secure pensions for Confederate veterans and kept meticulous records of his deeds with the Thomas Legion. (Courtesy of HCPL Digital Collection.)

THOMAS FAMILY AND NEIGHBORS. James R. Thomas (with black hat) and his wife (in front of the porch on the right) married in 1896 before moving to their new home in Waynesville, pictured here. Also in this *c*. 1906 image are the Thomas children, Josephine and James (in the buggy) and Dorothy, who stands directly in front of Anne Celleman, the family nurse. Other neighbors' children are clustered around Celleman. (Courtesy of HCPL Digital Collection.)

WAYSIDE LODGE. In the latter part of the 19th century, J. K. Boone and his wife lived for three years in this home, known as the Wayside Lodge. It operated as a boardinghouse, as many large homes in Waynesville did at the time. The Haywood County Courthouse looms in the background on the right. (Courtesy of Henry Foy.)

W. J. HANNAH. William Johnson Hannah (1867–1936), at right, was a Cataloochee-born Waynesville attorney who led a regiment of Haywood County soldiers in the Spanish-American War in 1898. Known as the Richland Rifles, they traveled by train to Raleigh with orders to sail to Cuba but were instead redirected to Camp Cuba Libre in Jacksonville, Florida. While stationed there for several months, Hannah came down with typhoid fever and had to relinquish his post as commanding officer for a month. By the end of the summer, he was back in good health. In December, he and his regiment received orders to sail to Havana, Cuba, where they took part in a flag-raising ceremony that officially concluded the end of the war with Spain. Below, he appears, seventh from right, with fellow officers of the war. Returning home to Waynesville, Hannah took up his law practice, married, got involved in local politics, and served a term as a state senator. He was also appointed the judge advocate general for Gov. Charles B. Aycock. (Both, courtesy of Bette Sprecher.)

BOONE-WITHERS HOUSE. Built around 1883 on Church Street, this prominent Victorian house was once the home of Jack Boone, a longtime Haywood County clerk of court. It later became a summer residence for James Grant of New Orleans. Under the ownership of Ernest Withers, the home became a hot spot for social events during the 1920s. (Courtesy of Henry Foy.)

COUNTY OFFICIALS. For more than two centuries, Haywood County's elected officials have convened in Waynesville to discuss the leading issues of the day at the county courthouse. Pictured here, from left to right, are W. A. Withers, county treasurer; Robert A. Hyatt Jr., clerk of superior court; Haywood County commissioners Joe Liner, William H. Leatherwood, Robert Q. McCracken, and Jim Boyd; C. Bonner Atkinson, register of deeds; and William J. Haynes, the county sheriff. (Courtesy of HCPL.)

JESSE DANIEL BOONE. An editor and publisher of Waynesville newspapers during the early 1900s, Jesse Daniel Boone wrote humorous rhyming poems on the front page of his weekly editions of the *Carolina Mountaineer and Waynesville Courier*. Offering fervent commentary on the issues of his day, he wrote editorials that supported the war effort during World War I. He also defended the Ku Klux Klan when the group met in Waynesville in the early 1920s. Boone sold his newspaper in 1925 to William Band. After a few more ownership changes, it found its present-day name, the *Mountaineer*. (Courtesy of HCPL Digital Collection.)

WAY HOUSE. Dr. Joseph Howell Way (1865–1927), the oldest of six children, was born in Waco, Texas. He moved to Waynesville in 1886 after studying medicine at the Medical College of Virginia and graduating from Vanderbilt University. He married Marietta Welch, the great-granddaughter of Robert Love, the founder of Waynesville. Way fathered several children who became leaders of the county and town, including son Jack Way, Waynesville's mayor for 28 years. In addition to being a prominent doctor in Waynesville, Joseph Way wrote for medical journals and served on a number of medical boards. He was secretary and president of the State Medical Society and secretary of the State Board of Medical Examiners. He also was appointed to the State Board of Health and the National Medical Congress. During World War I, he served as the chief medical officer for the Veterans Bureau Vocational School in Waynesville. His home, the three-story Queen Anne and Colonial Revival–style building known as the Way House (above) was built around 1895. It still stands on Main Street across the street from First Baptist Church of Waynesville. (Courtesy of HCPL Digital Collection.)

SHELTON HOUSE. In 1875, Stephen J. Shelton began construction on this home, above, using the walnut trees on his 67-acre property. He erected a two-story frame house with a two-tiered porch. A veteran of the Confederacy, Shelton also served as Haywood County's sheriff. After his death, his son William inherited the home, but the younger Shelton left Waynesville to follow a career working as an agricultural agent in New Mexico. William and his wife, Hattie, seated on the front porch, won many awards for their dahlias. In fact, William developed a special variety he named the "Hattie Shelton" in honor of his wife. After returning home in 1916, he set about adorning the Shelton House with many plants and flower gardens, seen below. The Shelton House was eventually sold and passed through a few owners before it became the North Carolina Museum of Handicrafts, with one of the best craft collections in the southeastern United States. The structure is on the National Register of Historic Places. (Both, courtesy of Shelton House.)

W. T. Crawford (1856–1913). Despite a limited early education, William Thomas Crawford (second from left) worked his way through local schools and graduated from Waynesville Academy at the age of 25. After jobs as a clerk and teacher, he developed a keen interest in debating and law, and eventually won a seat in the North Carolina House of Representatives in 1884. He served two terms before being elected as a U.S. Congressman in 1890. Winning four out of the seven times he ran for Congress as a Democrat, Crawford also ran a law office in Waynesville. He married Inez Edna Coman (second from right), who was a local advocate for women's rights. Together, they had seven children. (Courtesy of Bo Prevost.)

HON. JAMES M. MOODY

JAMES MONTRAVILLE MOODY. A Republican rival of W. T. Crawford and a fellow Waynesville attorney, James M. Moody was born in 1858 in Cherokee County (to the west of Haywood). His family moved to Jonathan Creek while Moody was a boy. After attending Waynesville Academy and the Collegiate Institute of Candler, he studied law, served as a prosecutor, and was elected to the state senate. He married Ellen Hawkins, the great-granddaughter of Holliman Battle, an early Waynesville businessman and state representative. By 1900, Moody ran for Congress, defeating W. T. Crawford. However, Moody's health declined soon after. He died in 1903 at his home. His funeral was attended by a congressional delegation that included 18 representatives and 5 senators. (Courtesy of HCPL Digital Collection.)

HERREN FAMILY REUNION. The Herren family gathered for a reunion at the original site of a log cabin built by their ancestor, Eli Herren. Behind the family, the National Hotel was built over and around the original family home and was run by the Herren family. Seated in chairs from left to right are Everette Miller; his spouse, Sally Herren Miller; A. Judson Herren and his wife, Jenny Herren; James Pickney; his wife, Molly Smathers Herren; and William Herren. They are surrounded by their children, nieces, and nephews. Among them is (second from right, first row) Lucille Herren, the youngest child of James Pickney and Molly Herren. (Courtesy of Henry Foy.)

HENRY FOY AND CHILDREN. Henry B. Foy Sr., who lived in Wilmington, North Carolina, when this *c.* 1926 photograph was taken, poses near the Herren House, a popular Waynesville boardinghouse. Beside him are Tommy Davis, Curtis Moore, and Foy's grandson, Henry Foy III (about two years old), who later became a longtime mayor of Waynesville. Moore was a grandson of Delsey Hackett, a cook at the Herren House. (Courtesy of Henry Foy.)

JOHN M. QUEEN. Born in 1881 and licensed to practice law in 1909, John Queen became Waynesville's first police court judge. He also served a two-year term as mayor of Waynesville during the terrible influenza outbreak of 1918. He died in 1958. The Queen family continues to play a prominent role in politics, with Joe Sam Queen, a Waynesville architect, currently representing the county as a state senator in the North Carolina General Assembly. (Courtesy of HCPL Digital Collection.)

TROOPS AT THE DEPOT. After the United States entered World War I, the men of Waynesville Company H of the First North Carolina Infantry were called up to defend America's border with Mexico. These soldiers departed from the Waynesville train depot on June 26, 1916, and were sent to France a year later. (Courtesy of Henry Foy.)

WORLD WAR I VETERAN. Thomas Guy Massie, left, served in France with the 6th Regiment of the U.S. Marines during the final drive that would defeat Germany in 1918. In a letter to his family in Haywood County, Massie described the intense fighting as the troops and tanks advanced, suffering heavy casualties. Though wounded by shrapnel in his head and leg, Massie would return home to help his father and brother run Massie Furniture in downtown Waynesville. The business still operates today on Main Street. (Courtesy of HCPL Digital Collection.)

OFF TO WAR. Before the United States declared war on Japan, Germany, and Italy in December 1941 and officially entered World War II, American men were being drafted into service. Dozens of draft announcements continued throughout the war. Here local residents gather outside the courthouse to see off new recruits. On the home front, local farmers produced greater yields for the war effort, and local factories such as the Dayton Rubber Company and Wellco ramped up production for military contracts. (Courtesy of HCPL Digital Collection.)

RETURNING VETERANS. Some students from Waynesville Township High School served in the military during World War II and returned home to high school after the war. As seen in this 1946–1947 school yearbook photograph, returning students included Wallace Anders, James Brackett, Odell Bradley, Harold Byrd, Hubert Caldwell, Mark Carswell, Robert Collins, Charles Crawford, Mark Dicus, Kenneth Dillard, Emmett Eller, William Fish, James Frady, Jack Fugate, Carol Grahl, Kent Ketner, William Liner, Boyd Medford, Tom Medford, Tom Messer, J. B. Miller, Fred Moore, Billy Pearson, Raymond Phillips, Jack Ramey, Frank Rickman, Charles Robinson, Howell Robinson, Walter Wyatt, Joe Milner, Joe Swayngim, and James Nicholas. (Courtesy of HCPL Digital Collection.)

Caroline Miller. The youngest of seven children born to a schoolteacher and a Methodist minister in southeastern Georgia, Caroline Miller (1903–1992) won the Pulitzer Prize in 1934 for her first novel, *Lamb in His Bosom*. The story captures rural, middle-class life in Georgia during the 19th century and defied Northern stereotypes that many in the South were either "poor white trash" or plantation owners. A star of the literary world at a relatively young age, Miller traveled widely and delighted audiences with her lectures. She vacationed in western North Carolina during the summers in the mid-1930s and eventually moved to Waynesville, where she remarried and settled down to raise a family with her new husband, Clyde Ray Jr., a local florist. Miller wrote a second novel, *Lebanon*, which was not as well received (it was severely cut, as paper was in short supply when it debuted in 1944 during World War II). Critics suggest Miller was overshadowed by another Pulitzer Prize-winning novelist from Georgia: Margaret Mitchell, author of *Gone With the Wind*. Nevertheless, Miller continued to write, garden, and help out with her husband's floral business on Main Street until her death in 1992. (Courtesy of HCPL Digital Collection.)

GIG YOUNG. Born in 1913 in St. Cloud, Minnesota, Byron Ellsworth Barr began a prodigious acting career in the early 1940s that spanned decades and dozens of movies and television shows. He was cast alongside such legends as Bette Davis, John Wayne, Cary Grant, Katharine Hepburn, Kirk Douglas, and Bruce Lee. Barr took his stage name from a character he played in the 1942 film *The Gay Sisters*, starring Barbara Stanwyck. The handsome, affable actor often sent hearts aflutter when he came to visit his parents in Waynesville. They moved to the small mountain town after Young's father took a job managing a local cannery. Though Young struggled with alcoholism and relationships, he found critical acclaim with an Academy Award and Golden Globe for Best Supporting Actor for his role as a seedy emcee named Rocky in the 1969 movie *They Shoot Horses, Don't They?* Young's life ended tragically in 1978 in a New York City apartment when he and his fifth wife, a 21-year-old German actress, were found shot to death. Young is buried at Green Hill Cemetery. (Courtesy of Bette Sprecher.)

FRED CRAWFORD. A Waynesville native and son of Congressman W. T. Crawford, Fred Crawford was the first athlete from North Carolina to be named to an All-American squad. Considered the top college lineman prospect in the South at the height of his career in 1933, he built a stellar reputation on the gridiron at Duke University, and his team narrowly missed making it to the Rose Bowl. Crawford later played a year with the Chicago Bears before a leg injury ended his pro career. Legendary Duke football coach Wallace Wade called Crawford "the greatest lineman I ever saw." (Courtesy of Bo Prevost.)

AIRMAIL. Local officials were on hand to see the first airmail delivered to Haywood County in the 1930s. The plane behind them landed on the ninth fairway of the Waynesville Country Club. From left to right are (first row) Canton mayor Paul Murray, Hazelwood mayor W. H. Prevost, Haywood County sheriff R. V. Welch, and Waynesville mayor Jack Way; (second row) Canton postmaster Wade C. Hill, pilot Paul McMurry, and Waynesville postmaster J. Hardin Howell. (Courtesy of HCPL Digital Collection.)

WINTER FUN. When it snows, sledding down the rolling hills at Waynesville Country Club was—and continues to be—a popular activity. In 1940, Laura Woody, in front of the sled, rode with her father, Jonathan Woody. Bobby Hardin looks on in the background. (Courtesy of Laura Soltis.)

41

AWARD-WINNING ARTWORK. The Pigeon Street School continues as a meeting place and cultural center for Waynesville's African American community. Here local residents display some of their award-winning crafts. From left to right are Elsie Osborne, a teacher and principal at the Pigeon Street School; Evangeline Gibbs, also a teacher at the school; Marion Howell; Juanitta Jackson; and Catherine Chapman. (Courtesy of Henry Foy.)

KIWANIS MEN. Social and civic clubs thrived in the mid-1900s in Waynesville. A group of men chartered the town's first Kiwanis Club in 1951 and helped sponsor various programs in the community. Waynesville's other civic organizations have included Rotary and Lions Clubs as well as the Women's Club, Jaycees, Toastmasters, and the Hazelwood Boosters Club. (Courtesy of Henry Foy.)

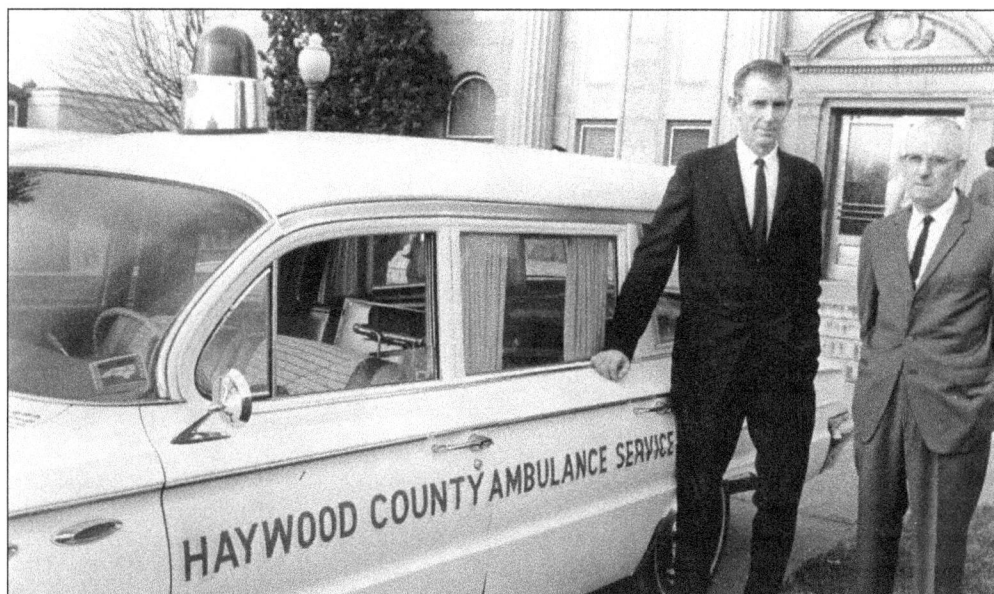

AMBULANCE SERVICE. The Haywood County Rescue Squad began in the 1950s after a girl drowned in Richland Creek. Her death moved local residents to provide a county-wide service that had not previously been available. In this image, Gene Howell (at left), a key player in starting the rescue squad, and George Brown, chairman of the Haywood County board of commissioners, stand alongside an ambulance in front of the county courthouse. (Courtesy of Henry Foy.)

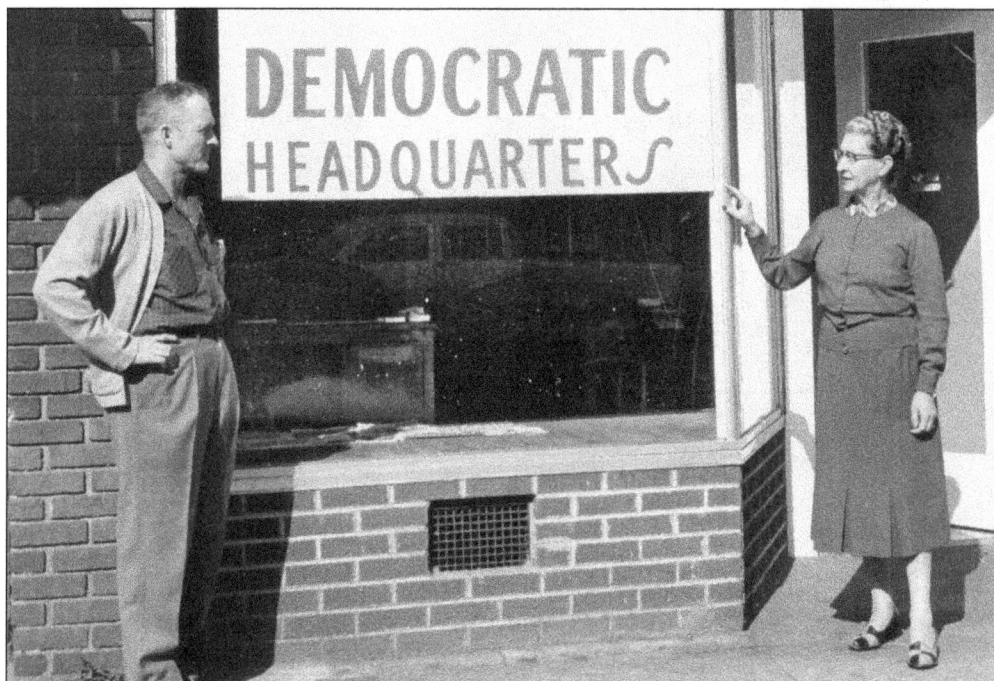

DEMOCRATIC PARTY HEADQUARTERS. Ernest Messer (left) and Edith Alley stand in front of the newly opened Haywood County Democratic Party Headquarters in downtown Waynesville (c. 1956). The Democrats have long held sway over the political scene in Waynesville and the surrounding county; since 1900, most local elections have favored them. (Courtesy of Henry Foy.)

WILLIAM GREER. Born the son of a farmer in County Tyrone in Northern Ireland, William Greer moved to the United States in 1929 and worked as a chauffeur for wealthy families in New York and Massachusetts. After serving in the navy during World War II, he joined the U.S. Secret Service in 1945, protecting Presidents Truman and Eisenhower. He was also the official driver for Pres. John F. Kennedy and Texas governor John Connally on the day of Kennedy's assassination, November 22, 1963. Afterwards Greer testified before the Warren Commission that investigated the events of that day. Despite the swirl of rumors and theories surrounding the assassination, neither Greer nor any other agents were found responsible for any wrongdoing. Greer retired from the Secret Service during Pres. Lyndon Johnson's term. He and his wife, Mary Finger Greer, moved to Waynesville in 1973. William Greer died in 1985 and is buried at Green Hill Cemetery. (Courtesy of Mary Finger Greer.)

LIONS CLUB. Members of the Lions Club of Waynesville are seen here around 1970. From left to right, they are (first row) Albert Wheeler, Lee Bouknight, Cleveland Martin, and Henry Dalton; (second row) Carl Bryant, William Howell, Junior Cullins, Charles Carrington, Thomas "Cowboy" Forney, Walter Bryson, and Jessie Scruggs. (Courtesy of the *Mountaineer*.)

FUTURE FIREFIGHTERS. The Waynesville Public Library has hosted many events for schoolchildren, including craft workshops, writing and reading activities, dance lessons, open mic nights, Quiz Bowl competitions, and Easter egg hunts. On a sunny July day in the 1980s, local children aided by the Waynesville Fire Department explored a fire truck, got to hold the fire hose, and used firefighter equipment. (Courtesy of HCPL.)

GEN. CARL EPTING MUNDY JR. A Vietnam War veteran with more than 41 years in the U.S. Marine Corps, Mundy served from 1991 to 1995 as the highest-ranking officer in the U.S. Marine Corps and a member of the Joint Chiefs of Staff. Born in Atlanta, Georgia, Mundy moved frequently with his family during his childhood and resided for several years in Waynesville during the 1940s and 1950s before moving back south to Montgomery, Alabama. After enlisting in the Marine Corps Reserve at the age of 18 and graduating from Auburn University, he went on to command and staff positions at every level. His military awards include 17 U.S. and foreign personal decorations and 10 unit and service awards. Carl III, his oldest son, was born and spent his formative years in Waynesville. Carl III also served as a Marine and was promoted to general, the first son of a Marine Corps commandant to do so. After retiring from the military in 1995, Gen. Carl Epting Mundy Jr. served as president and CEO of the worldwide United Service Organizations (USO). (Courtesy of Gen. Carl E. Mundy Jr.)

Three

STEEPLES AND STUDENTS

FIRST BAPTIST CHURCH. This church began congregating in 1823 in a log cabin along Richland Creek and then moved into a frame building on present-day Church Street. With the congregation expanding, a new church was built on the corner of Main and Academy Streets as seen above. The brick, Gothic building took five years to complete and opened in 1909. (Courtesy of the Shelton House Museum.)

JONES TEMPLE AME ZION CHURCH. At its original site, this church building stood on Green Hill overlooking Waynesville. Built in 1855, it was shared by Methodists, Presbyterians, and Episcopalians until those denominations built churches at other locations. In 1883, the building was moved to its present site just off Pigeon Street. In 1885, black members of Waynesville's Methodist church started their own congregation here in what is today the Jones Temple AME Zion Church. It is the oldest surviving church structure in Haywood County. (Courtesy of the *Mountaineer*.)

JONES TEMPLE TRUSTEES. Leaders of the Jones Temple AME Zion Church (*c.* 1981) included, from left to right, (first row) Agnes Bryson and Mag Lenoir; (second row) Hilliard Gibbs, Juanita Tate, and Roger Tate; (third row) Dennis Casey and Frank Burkes. (Courtesy of Lin Forney.)

Methodist Church & Public School, Waynesville, N. C.

Publ. by The Waynesville Book Co.

FIRST UNITED METHODIST CHURCH. Thanks to the missionary work of Bishop Francis Asbury, Methodism spread widely throughout western North Carolina in the 19th century. The First United Methodist Church of Waynesville, organized in 1831, moved to its present-day location, above, on Haywood Street in 1884. Located near the World Methodist Assembly at Lake Junaluska, the church often welcomes visiting ministers, missionaries, and bishops from around the world. In the picture below, taken in the spring of 1964, future U.S. vice president Hubert Humphrey (center door in the middle, facing left) visited First United Methodist Church. Rev. Horwood Myers, who was pastor of the church at the time, administered Holy Communion that Sunday. (Above, courtesy of HCPL Digital Collection; below, courtesy of First United Methodist Church.)

FIRST PRESBYTERIAN CHURCH. Organized in 1875 by the Reverend Alfred J. Morrison, this church congregation started with eight members. In 1880, the worshipers were given a lot on the corner of Main and Walnut Streets where a church was erected in 1882. In 1906, the framed structure was moved across the street temporarily to make room for the construction of the present-day church, above, which had yet to receive its windows and unique red tile roof. This church, dedicated in 1907, used an old, hand-pumped organ. Boys would pump the organ's side handle up and down to produce the air necessary to play hymns. At left, an inside view of the church shows the alcove behind the altar before it was filled with the pipes of a specially designed organ. (Both, courtesy of First Presbyterian Church of Waynesville.)

MAPLE GROVE CHURCH. In 1865, John H. Turpin founded an interdenominational church and school known as Turpin's Chapel. It has the oldest church-affiliated cemetery in the county. In 1910, a new, white building opened on the site as Maple Grove Church. Men of the congregation gathered for this photograph on its official christening. A fire in 1937 destroyed the building; a year later, the present-day brick structure was completed. (Courtesy of Maple Grove United Methodist Church.)

GRACE CHURCH IN THE MOUNTAINS. James Norwood and his wife held Waynesville's first Episcopal service in their home in 1847, with the Reverend James Buxton riding from Asheville to baptize their son. A charter, granted in 1868, formed a parish that shared a church building (at right) with local Methodists until the first Grace Church in the Mountains was constructed in 1878. This church would serve its congregation for 83 years before the present-day church building was erected. The Episcopal congregation in Waynesville has grown to be one of the largest in North Carolina, west of Asheville. (Courtesy of Grace Church in the Mountains of Waynesville.)

MOUNT OLIVE MISSIONARY BAPTIST CHURCH. At the close of the Civil War, newly emancipated African Americans in Haywood County began to form their own church congregations. What would become the Mount Olive Baptist congregation organized in 1869 and met on the third Sunday of each month in Waynesville's First Baptist Church. They built their own church in 1907 on donated land, which is the present-day site. The lovely Queen Anne structure features two front-side towers with open belfries and steep-angled pyramid roofs. (Courtesy of HCPL Digital Collection.)

MOUNT OLIVE BAPTIST CHURCH MEMBERS. On Men's Day, church members gathered for this *c.* 1975 photograph. From left to right are (first row) Hilliard Lee, Joe Simpson, Thomas Bryant Jr., Thomas Bryant Sr., Christopher Blount, Herman Gibbs, John Burnette, Thomas Churchwell, and Lee Bouknight; (second row) Odell Wilson, Clarence Thompson, Walter Haley, an unidentified visiting minister, the Reverend Frank Blount (Mount Olive Baptist Church pastor), Donald Forney, and Thomas "Cowboy" Forney. (Courtesy of Lee and Lorraine Bouknight.)

ST. JOHN'S CATHOLIC CHURCH. The small Catholic community in Waynesville, which began by worshiping in homes and in the ballroom of the Gordon Hotel, opened a school in the James Thomas home on Church Street in 1939. Five Franciscan nuns from Milwaukee ran the school. By 1943, it could accommodate students in kindergarten through 12th grade. Above are young students from a music class at the school. The image below captures a scene from a 1944 Christmas operetta set in a toy shop, complete with a proprietor, Dutch dolls, and toy soldiers. The auditorium where they performed seated about 50 people. (Courtesy of Laura Soltis.)

WAYNESVILLE GRADUATES. In the early 1900s, education beyond seventh grade was limited to a student's financial means and proximity of available schools. At the turn of the century, Waynesville officials passed a law for a local tax to build a new high school. Waynesville Township's first high school was housed in a local Masonic Lodge known as Waynesville Academy, located on the corner of Haywood and Academy Streets in the present-day Landmark apartment building. Above, graduating students pose in front of the school. Women were given flower bouquets along with rolled diplomas. (Courtesy of Henry Foy.)

WAYNESVILLE ACADEMY, 1914. Established in 1869, Waynesville Academy was originally located along the present-day Academy Street (hence the name). Here young students stand for a group photograph. Among them in the third row on the far right is William Hannah, a Waynesville attorney and father of former Waynesville alderwoman Bette Sprecher. (Courtesy of Bette Sprecher.)

FUTURE FARMERS. The Future Farmers of America began in 1928 as an organization dedicated to promoting farming and helping young men get started on agricultural careers. In the above image, the Waynesville Township High School's FFA club met in the Great Smoky Mountains National Park. Below, the 1951–1952 school officers sit for a photograph. From left to right are David Noland, secretary; Richard Hipps, reporter; Claude Caldwell, vice president; Frank Enloe, president; Ernest Inman, watchdog; and Jack Campbell, treasurer. (Both, courtesy of Laura Soltis.)

PIGSKIN LINE-UP. The Waynesville High School football team poses in preparation for the 1931 campaign. Glenn Wyatt (No. 2, standing at far left) would lead his squad to a first-ever upset over the Asheville High Maroons that year for the Mountaineers. Wyatt would score a touchdown in the final quarter to carry his team to a 7-6 victory. (Courtesy of Bobby Joe McClure.)

GIRLS BASKETBALL TEAM. Margaret Perry and C. E. Weatherby served as coaches for the Waynesville Township High School girls basketball team in the 1951–1952 school year. From left to right are (first row) Geraldine Keenum, Freida Ross, Nancy Leopard, Kathleen Creasmen, Mary Sue Sparks, Norma Winchester, Bobby Sparks, and Collie Reece; (second row) Sara Davis, Imogene Hooper, Fannie Kinsland, coach Margaret Perry, Shirley Jones, Linda Welch, coach C. E. Weatherby, Shirley Sheehan, Shirley Sheffield, and unidentified. (Courtesy of Laura Soltis.)

ARTISTIC EXPRESSIONS. In the 1940s, art was a new subject for students to pursue at Waynesville Township High School. The department started in 1943 when Inez Cloud Brooks taught the school's first art classes. The number of students who could attend art classes, however, was limited by the seating capacity of the two new workshops. (Courtesy of the HCPL Digital Collection.)

STANDING OUT. In 1946, Waynesville Township High School had only five graduating students. World War II drafts depleted many schools of teachers, staff, and students, but that is not the only reason the class of 1946 was so small. In the mid-1940s, the state's education system added a fourth year to high school, causing most of the class of 1946 to become the class of 1947. These five young women, however, put in enough extra time and studies to complete their four years' worth of schooling in three years. From left to right are Polly Dyer, Aletha Cagle, Frances Dyer, Billie McElroy, and Lena Frady. (Courtesy of HCPL Digital Collection.)

C. E. WEATHERBY. In 1929, Carlton Weatherby arrived in Waynesville to pursue a career in education. Fresh out of Duke University, Weatherby began at Waynesville Township High School. Over the years, he served as a social studies teacher, girls basketball coach, guidance counselor, and school principal. Weatherby's greatest impact, however, was made on the gridiron. He served as head football coach for 27 years, giving many inspirational speeches in the locker room. Upon his retirement, the Waynesville community named the school's athletic stadium after him, making C. E. Weatherby synonymous with football in Waynesville. (Courtesy of Bobby Joe McClure.)

Paper Bowl. Every autumn for over half a century, Haywood County residents have waited with high anticipation for the Paper Bowl, the evening when the rival teams from Waynesville and Canton battle it out on the football field. In 1951, the Waynesville Township High School Mountaineers, led by coach C. E. Weatherby, traveled to Canton with seven wins already under their belts. The Mountaineers had already squeaked out a 27-25 home victory over Canton earlier in the season, and huge crowds were on hand for the rematch. The Mountaineers shut out Canton in a 28-0 victory. Today's intra-county match-up continues to draw crowds of 10,000, whether it is played at Pisgah Stadium in Canton or C. E. Weatherby Stadium in Waynesville. (Courtesy of HCPL Digital Collection.)

ELSIE OSBORNE. In the days of racial segregation, African American students in Haywood County attended all-black elementary schools and did not have a county high school to attend until 1948. Elsie Osborne, above, served as a teacher and principal at the all-black Pigeon Street School in Waynesville. Though the U.S. Supreme Court declared segregation unconstitutional in 1954, the county did not desegregate its schools until the 1960s. (Courtesy of HCPL Digital Collection.)

SAM WHEELER JR. In August 1966, Haywood County's school system opened two integrated high schools—Pisgah High School in Canton and Tuscola High School on the western side of the county near Waynesville. Before that school year, Sam Wheeler Jr., left, and a dozen other black students transferred to Waynesville Township High School (the present-day site of Waynesville Middle School). Wheeler was the first and only black student to graduate from Waynesville Township in its final year as a high school. (Courtesy of HCPL Digital Collection.)

Four
OPEN FOR BUSINESS

HAT SHOP. Back in the days when hats were a popular piece of fashion, the best-dressed women in Waynesville came to a Main Street store run by Hattie Siler. She used velvet, silk, lace, ribbons, flowers, and feathers to decorate her hats and earned a stellar reputation for her artistry. A Haywood County native, Siler was a rarity in the early 1900s—a woman who owned her own business before women could vote. (Courtesy of Henry Foy.)

FIVE AND DIME. A. D. Simmons's Paris store was one of Waynesville's leading clothing shops for the first half of the 20th century. In the c. 1900 image above, a crowd of shoppers lines up on Main Street to take advantage of a 10-day sale featuring hats and clothes for women. (Courtesy of HCPL Digital Collection.)

PITCHFORD GROCERY. Grocery stores were a relatively new concept at the start of the 1900s in Waynesville. For decades, families supplied their food needs on their own farms, but as more people came to Waynesville, wholesale grocery stores found a niche. Early grocers not only sold household goods and basic staples, but also provided horse feed, hay, and agricultural supplies. (Courtesy of HCPL Digital Collection.)

WAYNESVILLE DISPENSARY. As a quaint ancestor of the modern-day pharmacy, this store sold a wide variety of items to heal or soothe physical ailments. The store closed in 1909. Note the dogs lounging in the back and a spittoon on the right side of the floor near a stool. (Courtesy of Hunter Library, Western Carolina University.)

WAYNESVILLE BOOK COMPANY. What started as a small newspaper and stationery stand evolved into a bookstore when H. C. Lindsley, a Minnesota native, bought the operation in 1900 and incorporated it as Waynesville Book Company in 1907. The store sold various genres of books as well as school supplies, office equipment, magazines and newspapers, postcards, and cameras. (Courtesy of Henry Foy.)

FROG LEVEL DEPOT. Passenger trains brought summer guests and traveling salesmen seeking relaxation, adventure, or business opportunities while they stayed at local boardinghouses and hotels. As Waynesville's transportation epicenter, the depot served not only as a point of entry and departure for business leaders, summer vacationers, soldiers, and local citizens, but was a hotbed of activity for bringing in new ideas and culture to what became a progressive town in the mountains. (Courtesy of Henry Foy.)

GARAGE. This Texaco garage station operated on the corner of Main and East Streets at the site of what is now the Waynesville Police Department. The business offered car parts, tires, tune-ups, gas, and even car storage. (Courtesy of Henry Foy.)

CRANE. Waynesville's Frog Level district remains a business community lined with the brick walls of industry. Some of the once-busy storefronts are vacant today, but the community has recently renovated several buildings. As a home to the Waynesville Depot, Frog Level saw all sorts of deliveries, as seen in this photograph. The crane is parked in front of Waynesville Wholesale Groceries, then owned by George Williamson. (Courtesy of Henry Foy.)

BRICK BY BRICK. Construction began on the new Haywood County Post Office in 1916. Above, laborers pause before a mountain sunset. To the left of the new structure is the Waynesville Hotel. The post office, completed in 1917, continued the growth and accessibility of mail for residents. Rural free delivery began in 1901. With new roads and new means of transportation, people throughout the county could receive letters, catalogs, and newspapers more easily. Today the historic brick building serves as the Waynesville Town Hall. Looking down the dirt road to the right in the photograph below is the neighboring C. E. Logan Auto Company, the first automobile in the county. (Both, courtesy Henry Foy.)

Main Street, looking South, Waynesville, N. C.

GROWTH OF MAIN STREET. A half-century of growth can be seen in these two images of downtown Waynesville. Above, the streets are yet to be paved, and power lines yet to be hung. The First National Bank stands prominently on the right. On the left of the street are H. C. Lindsley's Waynesville Book Company, drugstores, and grocers. Downtown also included a number of boardinghouses for summer guests and traveling salesmen. After an influx of business and industry arriving with the new rail service, Waynesville's downtown thrived, especially in the 1930s with the opening of the Great Smoky Mountains National Park. The sign in the image below stretched across Main Street to greet visitors and proclaimed the town's pride in being a gateway town to the national park. Dewey Stovall's shop appears on the right side of the street. American Fruit Stand, the next store down, was run by Dewey's brother Felix. On the immediate left, the Sinclair Gas Station sits on the site of the Kenmore Hotel, today occupied by a bank. (Both, courtesy of the HCPL Digital Collection.)

FOR MEN AND WOMEN
OF DISTINCTION.

Frank Ray & Co. have assembled a stunning display of Fall and Winter Ready-to-Wear Goods.

A COMPLETE LINE OF

Suits, Coats, Dresses, Red Cross Shoes Phoenix Silk Hosiery, Gloves, Neckwear, Underwear,	**FOR WOMEN**
Schloss Bros Clothes, Florsheim Shoes, Stetson Hats, Manhattan Shirts, Furnishings of all kinds.	**FOR MEN**

All New Goods---the latest products of the most fashionable shops---the last word in good form.

FRANK RAY & COMPANY
WAYNESVILLE, N. C.

CLOTHING ADVERTISEMENT. This 1916 advertisement for Frank Ray and Company of Waynesville included a small article proclaiming the store as the town's largest with two stories and a whopping 8,640 square feet of floor space. Organized in 1914 as an apparel store for men and women, it helped decrease "the shopping exodus" of local residents traveling to Asheville to buy fine clothes. (Courtesy of the *Carolina Mountaineer.*)

PARK THEATRE. By 1912, Waynesville had its first theater, the Waynewood. On Christmas Day in 1935, the Park Theatre, pictured here, opened with the feature film *Whipsaw*, starring Myrna Loy and Spencer Tracy. The building still stands as the Massie Mini-Mall on Main Street. (Courtesy of HCPL Digital Collection.)

SHERRILL STUDIO. George Sherrill learned about photography from his brother-in-law, Abraham Ensley, who lived in neighboring Jackson County. In 1902, Sherrill opened his own photography studio on Depot Street in Waynesville. It became a popular business for families and individuals who wanted photographic portraits. After Sherrill's death in 1931, his business passed on to his nephew, Ralph Ensley, and Ralph's wife, Beulah, who learned photography from Sherrill. The original stucco building with stone steps, above, was replaced in 1943 with a new structure closer to the ground level. (Courtesy of Henry Foy.)

LAP OF LUXURY. Mrs. Silverthorn, pictured here with a cozy kitty, ran a gift shop in downtown Waynesville that was named for her hometown of Aiken, South Carolina. The Aiken Gift Shop was located on Main Street, where Whitman's Bakery stands today. (Courtesy of Henry Foy.)

GARRETT FUNERAL HOME. Noble Garrett and his wife, Mary Lou, started Garrett Funeral Home in 1928. The home was situated one block west of Main Street. In 1942, the Garretts bought Massie Funeral Home, combining the two businesses. The company was sold to three employees in 1962. One of these employees was Ernest Edwards, whose family would go on to purchase Hillcrest Memorial Gardens on present-day Russ Avenue. (Courtesy of Mike McKinney.)

CRAWFORD FUNERAL HOME. In 1944, the Crawford family started a funeral home business in Clyde, just west of Waynesville. The following year, they opened a new location in Waynesville, purchasing the Stringfield home on Main Street, which was run by Ralph and Theda Garrett Crawford. The business and home remained until 1985 when it was bought out by Wells Greeley, a fourth-generation funeral home director of Wells Funeral Home, which started in Canton. The historic Crawford home was torn down in 1990 and replaced by the present-day Wells Funeral Home building in downtown Waynesville. (Courtesy of Wells Greeley.)

STANDARD OIL EXPLOSION. Early in the morning on July 14, 1942, Waynesville residents awoke to a thunderous explosion from a Standard Oil storage tank, located near the present-day Waynesville Middle School. Walter L. Hardin Jr., an agent for the company, discovered a leak on one of the tanks and alerted the Waynesville Fire Department. Thomas Taylor, a Standard Oil truck driver, went to go alert local residents of the impending danger, and Waynesville fire chief Lawrence Kerley climbed onto the leaking tank to seal the valve, but it was too late. The blast sent debris flying through the air and could be heard as far away as Maggie Valley. Kerley somehow survived the initial explosion but died several weeks later from his injuries. Hardin, Taylor, and another Standard Oil employee also died, along with Andy Caldwell; his wife, Leona; and their two children, who lived in a house near the oil tank. It remains Waynesville's deadliest disaster. (Courtesy of HCPL Digital Collection.)

BUSINESSMEN. For more than two centuries, business and politics have mingled in Waynesville. Leading businessmen—especially attorneys and physicians—have been among Waynesville's political elite. Seen here from left to right are a trio of Waynesville leaders from the mid-1900s: Waynesville mayor Jack Way, Haywood County commissioner Jim Boyd, and First National Bank president Jonathan Woody. (Courtesy of Laura Soltis.)

CHARLES E. RAY. A prominent Waynesville businessman in the first half of the 20th century, Charles E. Ray (center) ran a grocery store on the corner of Haywood and Church Streets where the present-day Waynesville Towers now stands. Ray served as a president of the county's chamber of commerce, led war bond drives during World War II, and donated the Shelton House in Waynesville. It became the North Carolina Museum of Handicrafts. (Courtesy of Shelton House.)

BUSINESS LEADERS. A year before Haywood County's 150th anniversary, business leaders had plenty to celebrate with the construction of Interstate 40, a major transportation route that ran west from Asheville, past Canton, and north of Waynesville. It would become one of the most important transportation developments for the county since the coming of railroad lines in the 1880s. (Courtesy of Henry Foy.)

WAYNESVILLE SKYVIEW, 1961. From its humble beginnings in 1810 as a sparsely populated frontier village, Waynesville has grown over the centuries into a modern town with access to a major interstate. The progress is visible in this aerial photograph overlooking Main Street and its northwest developments. Today a common destination for tourists, retirees, and second-home buyers, Waynesville continues to grow. (Courtesy of HCPL Digital Collection.)

TOWNE HOUSE. One of the finest restaurants in Waynesville, the Towne House earned an excellent reputation for its food and service. Owned and operated by Maude and Myrtle Jones and located next to the present-day First Presbyterian Church on Main Street, the eatery was a popular destination following church services. The business stayed in the Jones family, as it was passed down to a son and a daughter, Sam Jones and Catherine Honeycutt, before closing after a fire in the early 1970s. (Courtesy of Henry Foy.)

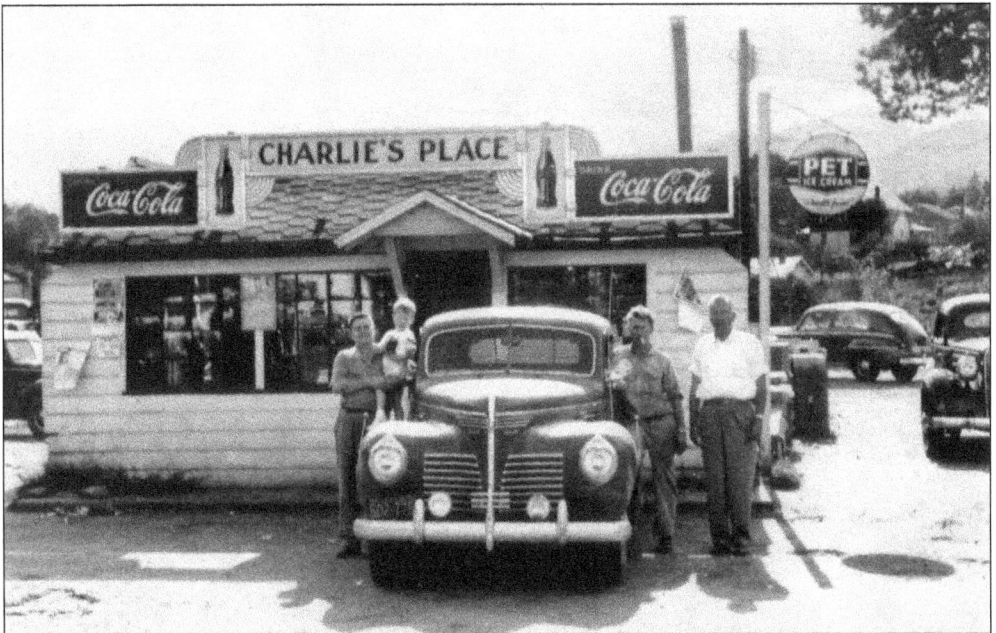

CHARLIE'S PLACE. In the 1930s, Charlie Woodard opened Charlie's Place restaurant, long a beloved, friendly destination in Waynesville. At its beginning the restaurant was open 24 hours a day. For more than 40 years, it served cheeseburgers, fries, and shakes to residents and visitors, young and old. Woodard retired in 1978 after selling his restaurant. Today Duvall's resides in the same familiar location. (Courtesy of Kim Crowe.)

HAYWOOD COUNTY HOSPITAL. This site became the first county hospital in the state built with funds from a county-wide bond referendum. It opened its doors on December 31, 1927. In 1979, the hospital relocated to its present-day site near Clyde and became Haywood Regional Medical Center. Today the former hospital building houses the Haywood County Schools administrative building. (Courtesy of HCPL Digital Collection.)

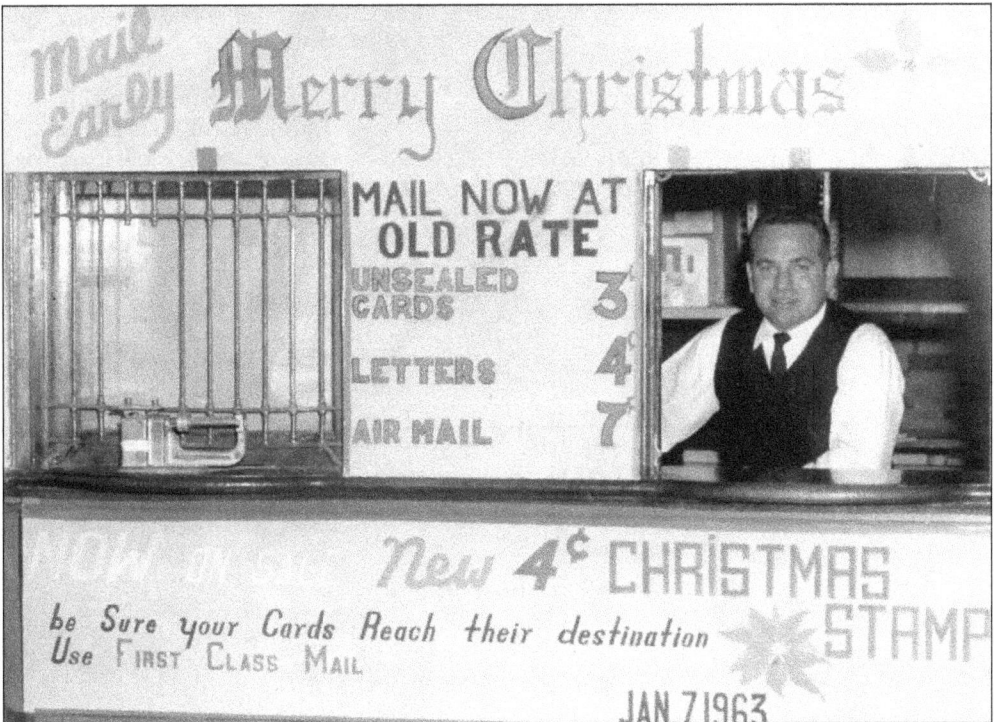

POST OFFICE CHRISTMAS. Waynesville's first post office opened in 1831, with rural free delivery beginning in 1901. By 1963, letters and cards could reach to their destination via airmail. Customers would stop at this post office location (present-day town hall) to send out their mail for as little as 3¢. (Courtesy of Henry Foy.)

ESSO MAN. As driving became more popular in the mid-1900s, the full-service auto station took its place in towns like Waynesville. At left is John Henry Foster, who worked at the Esso Station on Main Street in downtown, pumping gas and offering such services as washing windows and changing oil. (Courtesy of Henry Foy.)

CITIES SERVICE. Tom Lee ran the Cities Service station located on Main Street around 1950. The Waynesville station offered auto maintenance and an off-brand gasoline to motorists. On the left stands the LaFaine Hotel. Today the Justice Center sits on this location. (Courtesy of Henry Foy.)

WALL STREET. Waynesville town officials had this side street to downtown expanded in the fall of 1957. The street's name makes reference to the wall of buildings at the top of the hill where the road parallels Main Street. A few alleys connect the two streets, and a handful of Main Street businesses today have their lower levels on the Wall Street side. (Courtesy of Henry Foy.)

GIBBS PAINT AND BODY SHOP. Hilliard Gibbs Sr. opened the first black-owned business in Hazelwood in the 1960s. The automotive operation moved into a Waynesville building on Depot Street across from the present-day Walker Station and then once more to a structure on Wall Street behind the present-day Police Department. He retired in 1992. (Courtesy of Lin Forney.)

SCHULMAN'S. Dick Schulman and his wife opened a clothing store in nearby Canton in the 1960s before moving it to Waynesville in the 1980s. Situated in a building that was once the Royal Ice Cream Parlor, customers would travel from all over western North Carolina to shop at this upscale women's specialty shop. (Courtesy of the *Mountaineer.*)

BELK'S. Belk Hudson opened in town in the late 1930s with J. C. Jennings in management. After expanding, it was a large clothing store in the downtown Waynesville district. Belk Hudson relocated across town, atop a hill on Russ Avenue in the 1980s. (Courtesy of the *Mountaineer.*)

Five

HAZELWOOD

ALLENS CREEK. All of the naturally flowing water in Haywood County begins within its borders. On the western side of the county, waterways include Allens Creek, Plott Creek, and Richland Creek. Allens Creek, pictured here in this postcard, provides a pure water source for the people of Waynesville. Two of Hazelwood's earliest industries, the Quinlan-Monroe Sawmill and the Big Ridge Mica Mine, operated along its banks. (Courtesy of HCPL Digital Collection.)

MOUNTAIN VISTA. This tranquil 1947 view of Hazelwood belies its true identity as a bustling industrial town that included some of the county's largest employers, which produced textiles, rubber products, furniture, lumber, and shoes. These industries included the A. C. Lawrence Leather factory (rear right) and the Unagusta Furniture factory (rear center). (Courtesy of the *Mountaineer.*)

QUINLANTOWN. By 1900, train service brought a new industry to the Hazelwood community. E. E. Quinlan, a Pennsylvania businessman, and his son Charles began a sawmill operation that grew into a village known as Quinlantown, above. The company hired local farmers and loggers to harvest timber. By 1910, the community included 216 residents, several boardinghouses, a company commissary, a school, and various stores. The Quinlans started a furniture factory in Hazelwood that became Unagusta Furniture Company. (Courtesy of the North Carolina Office of Archives and History, Raleigh, North Carolina.)

TRAIN TO TOWN. Sawmill workers at Quinlantown built a tram to transport felled timber to the railroad and to furniture companies down the mountain. The flatbed cars seen here, loaded with lumber, would be guided down the wooden rails by a person with a brake in the rear car. Mules would be used to return the empty cars to the sawmill. Above, local residents relax on a sunny day ride. (Courtesy of the North Carolina Office of Archives and History, Raleigh, North Carolina.)

HAZELWOOD DEPOT. The train station in Hazelwood opened in the early 1900s, along a rail line that brought raw materials to the growing industries of Hazelwood. Residents now had a convenient way to travel, and passenger trains would continue to transport citizens of Hazelwood until the 1940s. The last Southern Railway passenger train passed through town in 1949. The depot would close to all rail traffic in 1964. (Courtesy HCPL Digital Collection.)

FUN IN THE SUN. Hazelwood attracted many families to the mountains, with parents seeking employment at the numerous industries in town. In this 1930s photograph, friends Ruth Marrow, Lucy Scates, and Lillie Wales of Hazelwood enjoy a day out together. (Courtesy of Hazelwood Baptist Church.)

UNAGUSTA. Employees of Unagusta Furniture Company in Hazelwood posed for this group photograph in the early 1900s. Incorporated in 1904, Unagusta began as an offshoot of the Quinlan-Monroe Lumber Company. The original factory was situated among abundant hardwood timber and next to new railroad lines. Begun with only 25 employees, the company would see tremendous growth, aided by its easy access to raw materials and its ability to construct a finished product on site. The factory built furniture, wooden columns, moldings, ceilings, floors, and wooden pipes. After a fire destroyed the plant in 1955, it was rebuilt at a nearby site and eventually sold to Lea Industries. (Courtesy of Bruce Briggs.)

A. C. LAWRENCE LEATHER COMPANY. Hazelwood's first major industry dates back to 1896, when the Junaluska Leather Company opened. Later renamed as the England Walton Company and then the A. C. Lawrence Leather Company, the tannery specialized in processing leather hides. Since the community did not have enough housing for its growing workforce, the leather company built homes for its employees. Many of these homes have since been torn down. Local men cut the nearby oak and chestnut bark, or "acid wood," and supplemented their incomes by selling it to the tannery. In 1931, the factory received shipments of hides to create products such as gloves and shoe soles. A. C. Lawrence Leather eventually closed its doors after nearly a century of leather production in Hazelwood. (Above, courtesy of HCPL Digital Collection; below, courtesy of the *Mountaineer*.)

ROYLE AND PILKINGTON. This company relocated to Hazelwood from New Jersey in 1928. At its outset, the Royle and Pilkington mill produced fine upholstery for the Pullman Car Company. After surviving the Great Depression in the 1930s, the business benefited from military contracts during World War II and contributed to the war effort by producing sturdy fabric for tents and sandbags. After the war, without updating its machinery and looms, the company could not compete with more modern textile mills. It ceased its operations in the 1960s and was later converted into a flea market space known as the Ragmill Mall. The building closed in 1970. (Courtesy of Bette Sprecher.)

A. L. FREEDLANDER. In 1919, A. L. Freedlander joined Dayton Rubber Company. A chemist and engineer, he played a major role in locating the rubber plant in Hazelwood in 1941. In his more than 52 years with Dayco, Freedlander contributed to the company's growth in the area and rose to the position of president and chairman of the board. He brought new laboratories to Waynesville, opening the Dayco Technical Center for research and development of diversified products. He also became a prominent local philanthropist, donating money to community organizations, most notably Haywood Community College. (Courtesy of HCPL Digital Collection.)

Dayco. In 1940, banker Jonathan Woody approached Fannie Boyd with inquiries into selling some of her land on Richland Creek to Dayton Rubber Company based in Ohio. On September 2, 1941, the talks came to fruition as the rubber manufacturing plant commonly known as "Dayco" opened its doors to 133 employees. Just over three months later, America's involvement in World War II began, and the plant commenced production, turning out oxygen masks and hoses, pontoon boats, life rafts, and other war-related products. The company's employees unionized in 1944, beginning a long tradition of great work benefits for local residents. After the war, Dayco diversified its production to include swimming pool hoses, vacuum cleaners, medical machines, and foam rubber products including mattresses. Because of this diversification, new research facilities moved into Waynesville. In 1985, Waynesville annexed the plant's property before the Dayco brand name and its rubber products were purchased by other companies. Dayco closed in October 1996 after 55 years of prosperity for Hazelwood and Waynesville. (Courtesy of Bruce Briggs.)

WELLCO. At the outset of World War II, Heinz Rollman fled Nazi-controlled Germany with his family and came to the United States. Looking for a business to use his shoe manufacturing patents, he found the Dayton Rubber Company in Hazelwood and started up Wellco Enterprises in 1941. Wellco eventually grew and established its own factory in Hazelwood. Rollman and his company originally produced slippers and casual shoes, but Wellco's subsidiary, Ro-Search, Inc., held valuable patents for attaching molded rubber soles to shoes and licensed these patents to other shoe manufacturers. Pictured above is Walter Kaufman, a cousin of Rollman, who became head of marketing at Wellco. Kaufman's son Rolf would go on to become a president and board chairman of the company. In 1965, the company acquired a contract to produce the first combat "jungle boot" for U.S. troops fighting in the Vietnam War. Although Wellco's operation has shut down in Hazelwood, the company continues to produce military, law enforcement, and sports footwear. (Both, courtesy of Rolf Kaufman and Wellco Enterprises.)

CLYDE'S RESTAURANT. Opened in 1941 across the street from what was once the Dayco factory, Clyde's has been a constant in the Hazelwood community and remains to this day. Clyde Green and Nivea Green served Dayco workers on their lunch breaks. In 1959, the restaurant opened the building seen above, and served two specials a day. The restaurant has remained in the family and is currently run by Van Green and his son Brandon. Clyde's continues to be a busy gathering place in town, its booths full of local residents enjoying good, quick meals. (Courtesy of Clyde's Restaurant.)

AMERICA'S PASTIME. In 1932, Hazelwood formed its own semiprofessional baseball team, the Hazelwood Manufacturers. The team played in the Western North Carolina Baseball League for many years. Above is a Hazelwood Manufacturers team from the 1950s. From left to right, they are (first row) Joel Burell and Bobby Kuykendall; (second row) Elmer Dudley, Sam Lane, Glen Wyatt, Jack Smith, Bud Blaylock, and Gene Wyatt; (third row) Steamer Harris, Bill Griffin, J. C. Burrell, Erun Shook, Gordon Wyatt, Stan Henry, Bill Milner, Babe Yount, and Pig Troutman. (Courtesy of Bobby Joe McClure.)

HAZELWOOD BAPTIST CHURCH. In 1917, Baptist worshippers from Hazelwood formed their own church under the Reverend W. M. Pruett with 50 charter members. Gathering in a shared school building on what is now Church Street for six years, the congregation eventually purchased a lot to build a church in Hazelwood. Completed in 1923, Hazelwood Baptist Church, above, was originally located on today's Camelot Street. After adding an education building in 1947, the church expanded and moved into the newly constructed present-day church structure on Hazelwood Avenue in 1958. (Courtesy Hazelwood Baptist Church.)

HOLY HARVEST. Various churches in the 1900s set aside a "Lord's Acre" or "God's Little Acre" to grow produce for their congregation and the community. In the c. 1950 photograph above, the Reverend M. L. Lewis (third from left) stands with members of his congregation from the Hazelwood Baptist Church. (Courtesy of Hazelwood Baptist Church.)

OFFICERS OF THE LAW. Four policemen stand in front of the present-day Hazelwood Baptist Church on Hazelwood Avenue. Shown here from left to right are Ricky Blanton, Kenneth Moore, Earl Robinson, and Ralph Pressley on Hazelwood's Main Street. (Courtesy of Hazelwood Baptist Church.)

HAZELWOOD PRESBYTERIAN CHURCH. In 1905, on the porch of a local home, the first Presbyterians of Hazelwood held services led by H. F. Beaty, a seminary student at the time. The lot for the church, right, was donated by Hazelwood's first mayor, E. E. Quinlan, in 1906. The congregation formed as the Hazelwood Presbyterian Church on November 9 of that year. After giving this building to a Methodist congregation, they began services in their present location in 1938. In the decades that followed, the church added a manse and an education building. (Courtesy of Hazelwood Presbyterian Church.)

HAZELWOOD SCHOOL. This new redbrick school built in 1923, on Virginia Avenue originally, contained 10 classrooms. By 1930, this second school, the Hazelwood School, was the largest in Waynesville Township. Over the next 45 years, the school would continue to add buildings and facilities. The school moved to a new location in 2004, and the original school building, shown here, is now used as the Folkmoot Friendship Center, headquarters for the international folk festival based in Waynesville. (Courtesy of Hazelwood Elementary School.)

GYM CLASS. Hazelwood School added a new playground after the purchase of a nearby lot, which allowed these students from the 1940–1941 school year to enjoy physical education classes. (Courtesy of Hazelwood Elementary School.)

HAZELWOOD CAFETERIA. Over the years, Hazelwood School added two additional buildings and purchased two acres of land for a playground. By 1953, there were more than 800 students with 22 teachers. In 1958, the school remodeled its cafeteria and installed new equipment. Above, students line up and receive their food in the updated lunchroom. (Courtesy of the *Mountaineer*.)

BROWNIES. The Girl Scouts established a Hazelwood chapter thanks to the Hazelwood Boosters Club. The organization provided young girls a chance to build friendships, boost self-confidence, and participate in community service projects. Here is Troop 87, a group of young scouts or "Brownies," in December 1958. (Courtesy of the *Mountaineer*.)

DAYTON RUBBER THOROUGHBREDS. Little League baseball in Hazelwood owes much of its formation to the Hazelwood Boosters. The first plot of land for a field was purchased in 1944 and dedicated in 1959. In this image, the Dayton Rubber Thoroughbreds pose for a team photograph after a winning season. (Courtesy of Ron Muse.)

CIVIL DEFENSE. The growing town of Hazelwood formed a Civil Defense Corps that was active at the end of the 1950s and early 1960s, at the height of the cold war. The uniformed corps was designed to help out in emergencies. In 1959, members toured area plants and factories to be prepared to aid in an emergency. Above are members of the Hazelwood Civil Defense Corps in 1960. (Courtesy of the *Mountaineer*.)

POST OFFICE DEDICATION. A new Hazelwood Post Office was opened on September 9, 1961. The new building replaced one that dated back to 1950. Here state representative Roy Taylor (left) presents a flag to Hazelwood postmaster Thurman Smith at the dedication. The Hazelwood Post Office, which still serves the community today, began home delivery in July 1961. (Courtesy of the *Mountaineer*.)

FOURTH OF JULY CARNIVAL. The Hazelwood Boosters Club sponsored a carnival every Independence Day, starting in 1946. Rides, food, and fireworks attracted people from all over the area. One contest offered a reward of $5 to anyone who could scale a greased flagpole to claim the prize. A favorite at every carnival was the carousel, shown here on July 4, 1961. (Courtesy of the *Mountaineer*.)

TOWN CENTER. In 1913, Hazelwood operated its first town hall in a feed store owned by J. S. Cowan, who added a room that year so the aldermen could meet there. A newer town hall, seen above in the 1950s, included the headquarters for other town services such as the police department, mayor's office, water department, and tax office. Hazelwood's government would move into a new home in 1978. (Courtesy of the *Mountaineer.*)

"I SOLEMNLY SWEAR." J. B. Siler administers the oath of office to four Hazelwood officials in December 1974. From left to right are Mayor Lawrence Davis, Mayor pro tem Glen H. Wyatt, and Aldermen Dr. Bill Prevost and Wallace Jones. This would be Davis's eighth and final term as Hazelwood's mayor, during which he would oversee the opening of the new town hall. Despite a stroke in August 1977, he continued to carry on his duties. (Courtesy of the *Mountaineer.*)

DOWNTOWN HAZELWOOD. The Hazelwood Pharmacy was a mainstay of downtown for nearly 50 years. Ralph F. Keenum (also known as "Little Doc"), Stuart Roberson, and Whitner "Red" Prevost formed a business partnership and opened the pharmacy in 1948. The pharmacy did a steady business, especially around noon when scores of factory workers put in orders at the lunch counter. Hamburgers were 25¢, milk shakes were 20¢, and banana splits were 35¢. On Sundays, customers could order 5¢ ice cream cones and 20¢ sodas. As a popular hangout for teenagers after school, the pharmacy kept a loyal customer base for decades. (Courtesy of the *Mountaineer*.)

PUBLIC SERVICE. The Fisher family has served the town of Hazelwood for three generations. C. L. "Dutch" Fisher, left, worked for the town as an alderman, filling the position of his father, F. Lee Fisher, who died in office. Dutch Fisher became Hazelwood's mayor in 1941 and served until 1951 and then again from 1959 until his death in 1972. The image below shows Dutch's daughter Mary Ann Fisher Enloe being sworn in as mayor of Hazelwood in 1983. While in office, Enloe wrote a grant to obtain land for a park named in her father's honor. Starting in 1948, community leaders began discussing plans for merging Hazelwood with Waynesville. Over the next five decades, the merger went to a referendum four times, but each time, it was defeated. Then in 1994, with some controversy and disagreement from residents, the vote was left up to the town governments, who approved the merger. Enloe was Hazelwood's last mayor when the industrial town officially became a part of Waynesville on July 1, 1995. (Both, courtesy of Mary Ann Fisher Enloe.)

Six

TOURISM

BATTLE HOTEL (OR BATTLE HOUSE). Holliman Battle, Haywood County's first postmaster and an early business leader in Waynesville, built a home at or near the present-day town hall and converted part of the house into a tavern for visitors. His son, Wayne Battle, added on to the structure to create a hotel that served guests for decades and was the site for one of the last Confederate surrenders of the Civil War. The hotel was torn down in the 1890s. (Courtesy of Henry Foy.)

WHITE SULPHUR SPRINGS HOTEL. In 1879, William Williams Stringfield and his wife, Maria, opened their Greek Revival–style home as a resort along what is now Sulphur Springs Road in Waynesville. Guests could enjoy fine dining and accommodations as well as croquet, tennis, billiards, dancing, hiking, and hunts into the nearby countryside. In its prime, the hotel could house about 250 guests. Prominent visitors included Stonewall Jackson's widow and a honeymooning Woodrow Wilson. The hotel also hosted the first organizational meetings for the North Carolina Association of Educators and the state's first chapter of the Daughters of the American Revolution. The hotel's original structure burned down in 1892, but its owners rebuilt it and added an annex. In 1918, the hotel and its grounds were converted into a military hospital for World War I soldiers suffering from tuberculosis and other respiratory ailments. Despite a number of renovations and reopenings, the resort never regained its former glory. It closed for good in 1927 and was demolished in 1941. (Both, courtesy of HCPL Digital Collection.)

SPRING HOUSE. The main attraction for guests at the White Sulphur Springs Hotel was a sulphur spring supposedly discovered on the property by a slave owned by James Robert Love, a son of Waynesville founder Robert Love and father of Maria Love—who married W. W. Stringfield. By the early 1900s, physicians touted health resorts for their healing, restorative qualities. Soaking in sulphur springs baths and taking in the cool mountain air were thought to ease symptoms of rheumatism, tuberculosis, skin disorders, and even insomnia. After a long, storied history, all that remains of Haywood County's first grand hotel is the spring house, seen above. In 1894, Waynesville's first telephone line was installed at J. P. Swift's livery stable on the corner of Haywood and Depot Streets. The line ran about a mile down the road to the White Sulphur Springs Hotel so that a saddled horse at the livery could be ready and waiting for hotel guests at a moment's notice. Below is the livery stable on the hotel grounds. (Both, courtesy of Hunter Library, Western Carolina University.)

WILLIS BOARDINGHOUSE. Waynesville's population would double, triple, or even quadruple during the summer months in the early 1900s. The incoming visitors would stay in the houses of local residents, who earned income by opening up their homes to summer guests. Rates per night might run from $1 to $2. The boardinghouse run by Emma Willis could accommodate 40 guests. A visitor would pay $2.50 a night or $10 a week. (Courtesy of HCPL Digital Collection.)

CROQUET COUPLE. A pair of guests lines up for some lawn croquet in the front yard of the Pinecrest, another boardinghouse in downtown Waynesville. Across the street in the back of this c. 1910 photograph is the First Baptist Church of Waynesville. (Courtesy of Henry Foy.)

GOING FOR A RIDE. Children of parents boarding in Waynesville sought out fun in various forms. In this 1920s image, a trio of young ones share a local pony on East Street leading into Waynesville's downtown district. (Courtesy of Henry Foy.)

HERREN HOUSE. Cats and boarders were both welcome at this prominent boardinghouse in Waynesville. Jessie Herren, left, ran the house and later took over the Hotel Waynesville on Main Street. Cats proved quite useful to boardinghouse owners in getting rid of unwanted rodents and were rewarded with food scraps for their services. (Courtesy of Henry Foy.)

ES NEST HOTEL—ELEVATION FIVE THOUSAND FEET. TWO THOUSAND FEET ABOVE "WAYNESVILLE THE BEAUTIFUL" BUT THIRTE
HUNDRED FEET BELOW PLOTT AND JONES' PEAKS. MAGNIFICENT DRIVE OF FIVE MILES UP JUNALUSKA MOUNTAIN—VIEWS FROM
HOTEL AND DRIVE ARE ONE BEYOND DESCRIPTION. "SURPASSES SWITZERLAND IN VASTNESS" SAID AN ENGLISH TRAVELER

EAGLE'S NEST HOTEL. This grand hotel, built in 1902 on a Junaluska Mountain perch 5,050 feet above sea level overlooking Waynesville, featured three stories, 50 rooms, a grand lobby with a roaring fireplace (four in all), an observation tower, and a wraparound porch. Summer guests engaged in dancing, card games, fine dining, fancy parties, and hikes around the nearby countryside. Just before the summer season began in 1918, a fire broke out at the hotel. The secluded reach of the inn turned out to be a curse, as fire crews could not reach the hotel in time to save it from utter destruction. The owner, S. C. Satterthwaite, declined to rebuild, but local residents would eventually refer to this mountain as Eagles Nest. (Courtesy of Henry Foy.)

HOTEL WAYNESVILLE. Built in the late 19th century between the old Dunham House and the Waynesville Town Hall, the three-story inn seen above featured a first-floor veranda with flattened arches, balcony porches on the second and third floors, and a tower (on its left side). The hotel was torn down in the 1930s. In the photograph at right, owner Jessie Herren finds some quiet time to read inside her hotel. (Both, courtesy of Henry Foy.)

NEW DEAL, NEW PARK. In the midst of the Great Depression, Waynesville residents strongly supported Franklin Delano Roosevelt and his administration's New Deal programs. The Civilian Conservation Corps and the Works Projects Administration brought jobs to the area as workers built new schools, bridges, and roads. The town received federal funds for the construction of the present-day historic courthouse during the New Deal. With the creation of the Great Smoky Mountains National Park and the Blue Ridge Parkway in the 1930s, Waynesville became a gateway to two nationally recognized tourist attractions. In 1936, Roosevelt (seen below waving his hat) visited Waynesville to celebrate the opening of the Great Smoky Mountains National Park, which is today the most visited national park in the United States. (Both, courtesy of HCPL Digital Collection.)

DOROTHY DIX. One of the most popular journalists of the early 1900s, Dorothy Dix (center, in floral dress), was the pseudonym of Elizabeth Meriwether Gilmer. She wrote an advice column on love and marriage that was read by millions worldwide. Dix visited Haywood County in 1940 for a tour of the newly established Great Smoky Mountains National Park. Pictured here are, from left to right, Great Smoky Mountains Park superintendent J. Ross Eakin, Ann Watkins, Mrs. Rufus Blackwell, Dix, Mrs. S. P. Gay, Mrs. Ferguson, and her husband, Gen. Harley Ferguson. (Courtesy of Shelton House.)

WAYNESVILLE COUNTRY CLUB. Jim Long began this country club in 1926 on land that was once owned by dairy farmer Frank Welch. In 1930, Long had a Colonial Revival–style lodge built. The original nine-hole golf course was expanded to 18 holes in 1935. The first professional golfer at the club was John Drake. (Courtesy of HCPL Digital Collection.)

SUYETA PARK HOTEL. Constructed in 1909 for R. D. Gilmer and his family, the three-story main building and two-story annex included rooms for 125 guests. The annex served as the home for the Gilmer family. It featured a wraparound porch with dual Tuscan columns, gabled bay windows, a large living room, an ornate stairway, marbled mantelpieces, and finely carved woodwork. Its unique name—Suyeta—means "the chosen one" in Cherokee. (Courtesy of HCPL Digital Collection.)

THE GORDON. Boasting beautiful views in every room and the finest cuisine, the Gordon Hotel was known in the early 1900s as one of the leading grand hotels of the region. Built in the early 1890s and expanded to include a third floor, private baths on the second floor, a ballroom pavilion, and interior touches like a birch staircase, the Gordon was purchased in 1912 by a Florida businessman named F. O. Dunham, who also purchased the Dunham House in Waynesville. After Dunham's arrival, guests of the Gordon could enjoy an orchestra for dinner music as well as social dances (some with costumes). The hotel's own dairy supplied fresh milk, and a large dining room could seat 100 people. The Gordon suffered a fire in 1957 and was demolished soon afterwards. By then, interstate travel and cheaper hotels spelled the demise of many grand hotels that once reigned over the local landscape. (Courtesy of Henry Foy.)

THE KENMORE HOTEL. This 40-room, two-story building on Main Street included a pyramid roof with a flattened peak, a small turret, a small porch on the second floor, and a wraparound porch on the bottom floor. In its later years, it fell into disrepair and its front porch was converted into a grocery store. (Courtesy of Henry Foy.)

ADGER HOUSE. Built around 1900 as a large summer home for a Charleston woman with the last name of Adger, the home is within a moderate walk from downtown Waynesville. The Colonial Revival architecture, with its two-story columns and wide front porch, seemed the perfect picture of summertime relaxation. Up until recent years, it continued to welcome guests as a bed and breakfast but is now a private residence. (Courtesy of Adger House.)

THE LINGAMORE, EAGLES NEST ROAD, WAYNESVILLE, N. C.

LINGAMORE HOTEL. Owned by the Hyatt family and developed at the end of the 19th century, the Lingamore was actually a series of three homes with a spacious front lawn, set back from Eagles Nest Road. A 1.5-story frame structure, built in 1896, was used as a residence and dining hall in the summer. The other two-story buildings were also private homes that opened to summer guests. (Courtesy of HCPL Digital Collection.)

LAFAINE HOTEL. First known as the Windsor Hotel, the LaFaine was located on Main Street between the present-day First Presbyterian Church of Waynesville and the Haywood County Courthouse. Unlike some of the grand hotels along Main Street, the LaFaine was a modest building with inexpensive rooms. It outlasted many of the larger inns before it was demolished in 1980 to make room for a courthouse parking lot. (Courtesy of HCPL Digital Collection.)

INTERNATIONAL FESTIVAL DAY. On the last Saturday of Folkmoot, a two-week international dance and music festival held in Waynesville each summer, the downtown district from town hall to the county courthouse is blocked off to create a world bazaar with artisans and crafters from the region mingling with visiting dance troupes from across the globe. Past performers have included stilt dancers from France, theatrical drummers from Japan, and hula dancers from New Zealand. International Festival Day is traditionally the largest single-day tourist event in the county. (Courtesy of Haywood County Arts Council.)

Seven

ARTS AND LEISURE

WOOLSEY HEIGHTS. Methorn Woolsey owned a 30-acre estate to the northeast of downtown Waynesville. Woolsey's two daughters each received a 2.5-story house on the grounds, erected on either side of his. The rolling mountains also featured a private swimming pool offered to friends on a lazy summer day. The houses built by Woolsey still stand today. (Courtesy of Henry Foy.)

WAYNESVILLE FAIRGROUNDS. David Russell Noland helped spearhead the first Haywood County Fair held in Waynesville in 1905. The fair, pictured here, showcased locally made crafts and hundreds of agricultural exhibits, including livestock and bounties of apples, pumpkins, corn, berries, and grains. Cash prizes went to the top winners in various categories. Local residents would ride or walk for hours to the 20-acre fairgrounds, pictured above, located along Smathers Street in Waynesville. Admission was 50¢ a day or $1 for the whole fair. Main attractions included horse races, Ferris wheel rides, and automobile rides. However, critics decried the shady elements of the fair, including gambling, drunkenness, and immodest ladies dancing for men-only shows. The fair eventually closed in 1915. Organizers tried to bring it back in the 1930s, but it was deemed too expensive. Several more attempts sputtered until 1990 when the county purchased a fairground property off NC209 near Lake Junaluska. (Courtesy of Henry Foy.)

DIAMONDS AND DUGOUTS. Waynesville has fielded baseball teams for well over a century, including this one from *c.* 1900. In addition to the teams sponsored by local businesses and factories in the Waynesville and Hazelwood communities, some teams formed to compete in statewide tournaments. (Courtesy of Louise K. Nelson.)

MOUNTAIN SCOUTS. A Boy Scout troop from Waynesville gathers on the steps of the Haywood County courthouse in 1914. Scoutmaster W. C. Allen stands to the right of the scouts. Allen, a longtime Waynesville professor and a superintendent of Waynesville schools, wrote numerous histories of the county that are still used today. From left to right are (first row) an unidentified scout, Phil Blackwell, Hugh Campbell, Lloyd Whitier, Dick Covington, and Melvin Reeves; (second row) Fred Love, two unidentified scouts, Curtis Logan Jr., Bryan Reeves Jr., Baisel Morrison, and Gladsom McDowell. (Courtesy of the Shelton House.)

PARADE CART. Workers from A. C. Lawrence Leather, a tannery in Hazelwood, prepare for a local parade during World War II. Their patriotic buggy encourages onlookers to purchase war bonds. Waynesville and Hazelwood businesses and citizens exceeded the financial goals set during several war bond rallies, raising hundreds of thousands of dollars for U.S. military efforts overseas. (Courtesy of HCPL Digital Collection.)

APPLE FESTIVAL. This 1957 Apple Festival Parade down Waynesville's Main Street spotlighted one of the region's most abundant crops. Apple orchards have long thrived in the cool climate of western North Carolina, and Waynesville still celebrates the fall harvest season with delicious apple varieties, apple treats, cider, and savory apple-related recipes. (Courtesy of Henry Foy.)

116

CHRISTMAS PARADES.
Waynesville's downtown
Main Street is a perfect
lane for a parade.
The town has held
parades to rally people
in wartime, celebrate
holidays and festivals,
and promote local
businesses. High school
marching bands, floats,
and dancers highlight
the procession as the
community comes
together. Main Street is
also the gathering spot
for numerous festivals,
craft shows, music,
and street dancing. At
right, local Girl Scouts
make their way past the
courthouse in a 1950s
Christmas parade. In
the image below, a
children's float from
Hazelwood passes as the
twirling Mountaineer
majorettes follow. (Both,
courtesy of Henry Foy.)

BOOKMOBILE. In the 1940s, Haywood County began to receive state funds to expand its library services. The library also raised $3,000 through events such as penny drives and musical concerts to purchase a bookmobile. In 1948, the bookmobile, based at the public library in Waynesville, began making stops throughout the county at homes, schools, and businesses. (Courtesy of HCPL.)

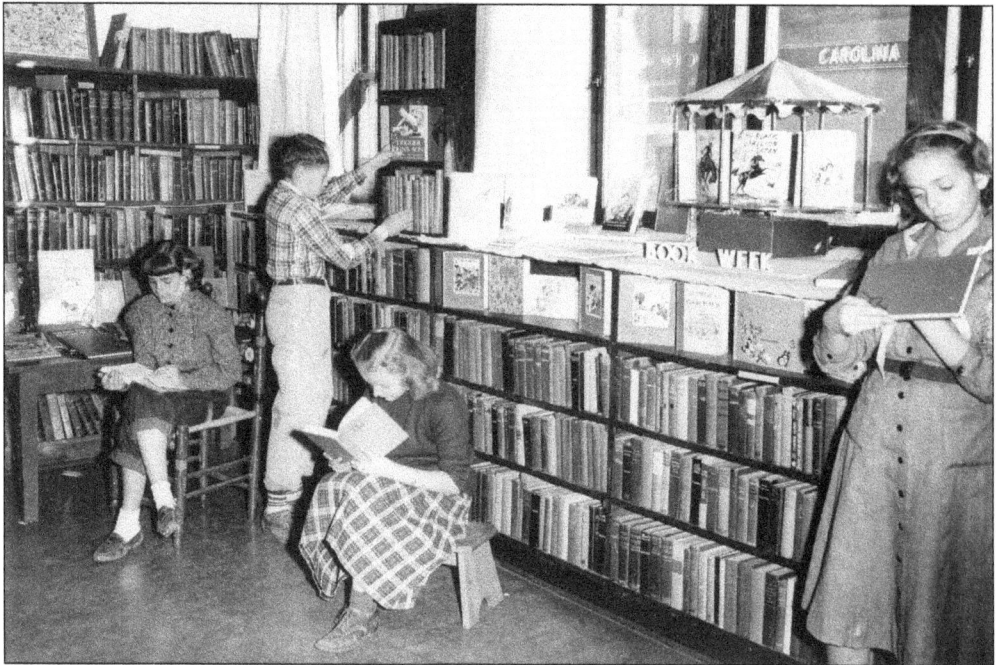

ALL BOOKED UP. The library in Waynesville can trace its roots to the 1890s when residents gathered to invest in a community building. The first library was established above the office of W. B. Ferguson, a lawyer on Main Street. After moving to the upper floor of another local business, the library's directors purchased the rock building on Main Street, which opened in 1940 as a public library, seen above. The library would eventually move into W. B. Ferguson's house in 1955 and then to its current location in the early 1980s, remaining on the Ferguson property. (Courtesy of HCPL.)

Holiday Giving. Waynesville has a long history of helping residents in need, dating back to the establishment of the town welfare department in 1919. Here, in the county courthouse in downtown Waynesville, women prepare to hand out toy trucks to children for the holidays. (Courtesy of Henry Foy.)

Tea, Flowers, and Cake. Margaret Johnston, standing in the center, was Waynesville's first full-time public librarian. Upon her arrival, she began to promote the library's services through events such as tea times. She also pushed for a new, more adequate library building. Sarah Thomas Campbell sits to her right. (Courtesy of Henry Foy.)

SHEREE WHITE SORRELLS. A prominent textile artist who once operated a studio in downtown Waynesville, Sorrells is a member of the prestigious Southern Highland Craft Guild. Her rag rugs and weavings have been exhibited in national craft council shows and museums and featured in state and national magazines. (Courtesy of Haywood County Arts Council.)

BURR STUDIO. MaryEtta Burr and her husband, Dane, have operated their art gallery and studio in downtown Waynesville for decades. MaryEtta, who graduated from Ohio State University, creates wheel-thrown, mostly functional pottery, while Dane, a graduate from the Cleveland Institute of Art, is a sculptor and visual artist who produces playful, exotic animals like echidnas. (Courtesy of Haywood County Arts Council.)

TERESA PENNINGTON. A self-taught colored pencil artist, Pennington and her downtown Waynesville gallery have been a mainstay for a number of years. She has been commissioned by the Biltmore Estate, the Blue Ridge Parkway Foundation, and the U.S. Forest Service to draw flora, fauna, and mountain landscapes. (Courtesy of Haywood County Arts Council.)

DIANNAH BEAUREGARD. Growing up with a love for nature and minerals, Diannah Beauregard has always been intrigued with gems. In 1983, she moved to Haywood County to study jewelry in the Haywood Community College Production and Crafts Program, a nationally recognized program that equips craft artists to make and market their work. She designs award-winning customized pieces and contributes proceeds from artwork to help support local causes. (Courtesy of Haywood County Arts Council.)

STRAND THEATRE. Once a movie theater and then a stage for local community plays, the Strand Theatre on Main Street carries a lot of memories of bright lights and big dreams. Built in 1946, the building served as a movie theater until 1980. Haywood County thespians formed the Haywood Arts Repertory Theatre (HART) in 1985 and found a home at the Strand for nine years until the building was deemed a fire hazard. HART performed its plays at Haywood Community College's auditorium for a time before its present-day facility was built on the grounds of the Shelton House. Decades after it was abandoned as a theater space, various business ventures have sought to renovate the old Strand and return the movie theater to its former glory. (Courtesy of Haywood Arts Regional Theatre.)

THE RAINMAKER. Steve Lloyd (kneeling, center) came to Haywood County as a visiting artist at Haywood Community College from 1988 to 1990. An actor and playwright with off-Broadway appearances, Lloyd found a home with the Haywood Arts Repertory Theatre in 1990 (later renamed the Haywood Arts Regional Theatre) and has served as the organization's executive director ever since. Over the past two decades, he has directed dozens of shows and starred in some as well. He has also championed community theater as a statewide president of the North Carolina Theatre Conference. (Courtesy of Haywood Arts Regional Theatre.)

HART Performing Arts Center. This rustic, multi-gabled facility designed by Waynesville architect Joe Sam Queen features a 300-seat main auditorium, an orchestra pit, dressing rooms, a 75-seat studio theater, offices, and a lobby that presents monthly art exhibits. Completed in 1994 on the grounds of the historic Shelton House and paid for through generous public donations, the facility is one of the most active community theaters in the Southeast with six main stage shows, a series of studio theater shows, music concerts, festivals, and receptions scheduled throughout the year. (Courtesy of Haywood Arts Regional Theatre.)

Thespians. Mary Roadruck, left, and Steve Wall, right, perform in HART's 1991 production of *Man of La Mancha*. Roadruck, who taught drama at Tuscola High School, and Wall, a Haywood County pediatrician, are among hundreds of local actors who have volunteered in HART shows over the years since the theater's founding in 1985. HART productions have won state, regional, and national honors at theater festivals. (Courtesy of Haywood Arts Regional Theatre.)

BOWLING TEAM. Waynesville recreation has not solely consisted of competition on ball fields and courts. The Gibbs Paint and Body Shop in Hazelwood sponsored this bowling team, seen here around 1962. From left to right are Jackie Bryant, Doyle Gibbs, James Bryant, Jacob "Buzz" Lenoir, and Hilliard Gibbs. (Courtesy of Lin Forney.)

TIME CAPSULE. Waynesville celebrated the centennial of its incorporation in 1971 by burying a time capsule in front of the present-day town hall. C. C. Francis, chairman of the county commissioners, digs at center. Sarah Thomas Campbell stands next to Francis in a traditional dress. Waynesville police chief Arthur Paul Evans stands to the far right. Ray Rouser stands in the back with a hat. (Courtesy of Henry Foy.)

RAMP FESTIVAL. Each year in May, Waynesville hosts a unique festival dedicated to the ramp, a locally grown pungent cousin of the onion. The tradition started at Black Camp Gap near Maggie Valley in 1932. Residents there would harvest ramps and cook them over campfires. The festival eventually moved to Waynesville where it became even more popular, with music, visiting politicians, ramp-eating contests, and various dishes using ramps. (Courtesy of the *Mountaineer*.)

HAYWOOD COUNTY ARTS COUNCIL. Since its incorporation in 1977, the Haywood County Arts Council has operated out of several locations, including the Canton Armory, the Federal Building in Waynesville (shown above), the old Masonic Temple building on Church Street, and its present-day site at 86 North Main Street. Pictured here are some early leaders of the arts council. From left to right are (sitting) Paula McElroy, Terry Painter, Jean Anne Wells, James Roy Moody, and Libba Feichter; (standing) Brewster Ward, Suzanne Tannehill, Helen Howie, Ron Huelster, and Ed Nash. (Courtesy of Haywood County Arts Council.)

FOLKMOOT, USA. What began as a cultural celebration in Waynesville in 1984 has blossomed into one of the region's most popular annual events, drawing thousands of tourists and pumping millions into the local economy. Founded by a Waynesville physician named Clinton Border, the festival got its name from an Old English word meaning "a meeting of the people." Each summer, for two weeks in July, 10–12 visiting folk dancing troupes and accompanying musicians perform in venues throughout the region. They are housed at the Folkmoot Friendship Center (formerly Hazelwood Elementary School). The festivities kick off with a Friday Parade of Nations down Waynesville's Main Street and feature dozens of performances before concluding with a final show from each of the visiting groups and a Candlelight Closing at Lake Junaluska's Stuart Auditorium. In its 26-year history, the festival has welcomed more than 200 folk groups from more than 100 nations who come to share their musical and dancing traditions in a spirit of international peace and friendship. Above, a dancer performs in front of the Haywood County Courthouse. (Photograph by Jan Collett; courtesy of Haywood County Arts Council.)

BIBLIOGRAPHY

Allen, William Cicero. *The Annals of Haywood County, North Carolina.* Spartanburg, SC: The Reprint Company, Publishers, 1977.

Anderson, Nina L., and William L. Anderson. *Heritage of Healing: A Medical History of Haywood County.* Waynesville, NC: Waynesville Historical Society, 1994.

Crow, Vernon H. *Storm in the Mountains: Thomas' Confederate Legion of Cherokee Indians and Mountaineers.* Cherokee, NC: Press of the Museum of the Cherokee Indian, 1982.

Farlow, Betsy, et al. *Haywood Homes and History.* Hazelwood, NC: Oliver Scriptorium, 1993.

Haywood County Genealogical Society. *Haywood County Heritage, Vol. 1.* Marceline, MO: Walsworth Publishing Company, 1994.

Nelson, Louise K. *Historic Waynesville and Haywood County: What was it like?* Waynesville, NC: self-published, 1999.

Oliver, Duane. *Mountain Gables: A History of Haywood County Architecture.* Waynesville, NC: Oliver Scriptorium, 2001.

Webb, Janet Threlkeld. *Haywood County: A Brief History.* Charleston, SC: History Press, 2006.

Wood, Curtis, ed. *Haywood County: Portrait of a Mountain Community.* Greenville, SC: Southern Historical Press, 2009.

Visit us at
arcadiapublishing.com

www.ingramcontent.com/pod-product-compliance
Lightning Source LLC
Chambersburg PA
CBHW050609110426
42813CB00008B/2505